# PREFACE

Back in the early 50's, when I was about ten years old, I saw my first picture of an iguanid—it was a black and white picture among lots of other reptile pictures in the back of Raymond L. Ditmars's book *Reptiles of the World*. The picture made me a case of ordering Ditmars's book through the public library. Nowadays, I actually have my own copy of it; in fact I have a whole library of interesting herpetological works and have been involved with herpetology in a greater or lesser degree for most

ISABELLE FRANCAIS

Of all the iguanids, the Green Iguana, *Iguana iguana*, is undoubtedly the most popular among herpetoculturists. Inexpensive, attractive, and hardy, Green Iguanas make very good pets.

want to own an iguanid more than any other thing in the world, but it was to be another 14 years before this ambition became a reality.

I, like many budding herpetologists both amateur and professional, had been deeply influenced by Ditmars's book. At that time, I had already passed the "snail in the bottle stage" and had graduated well into the "treefrogs and Italian Wall Lizards in glass tanks" mode. Unfortunately, in those days there was very little popular literature on keeping such "creepy crawlies" as pets, and it was

of my working life. Much of this can be blamed on that early black and white picture of an iguanid!

The iguanid that springs to my mind most often is the big Green Iguana, *Iguana iguana*, of Central and South America. This species has been a well-loved terrarium subject for decades. In the early years of terrarium keeping, many Green Iguanas died after only a few weeks in captivity, largely due to ignorance on the part of the keeper. However, the experience of all keepers over the decades has resulted in state-of-the-art husbandry techniques that allow these fascinating creatures to live long and happy captive lives and even reproduce.

The Green Iguana, however, is but one species in a family containing around two dozen. In this book we will be discussing the iguanids as whole, then "zero in" on the popular and much-loved Green Iguana in a special chapter all its own.

With regard to many wild species of iguanids, the present situation is a sad one. Not only is the Green Iguana, for example, still heavily exploited for the pet trade, it is also considered a delicacy by those who live in its range. This, coupled with a deadly demon known as habitat destruction, has led to a serious decline of the overall Green Iguana population. In some areas, only a fraction of the population that existed 50 years ago still remains. Every keeper of Green Iguanas should make it a priority to try breeding his or her specimens. Every captive-bred specimen will mean one less collected from the wild. It is hoped that captive-breeding will lead to self-sufficient captive populations, thus precluding the need to take specimens from the wild.

Whatever the future holds for iguanids, or for nature in general, the terrarium keeper does have a part to play in promoting an awareness toward the diversity of life and the importance of maintaining it. It is hoped that this book will introduce the budding "iguanaphile" to many years of interest and pleasure!

**John Coborn**
*Nanango, Queensland, Australia*

A most fascinating iguanid, the Chuckwalla, *Sauromalus obesus*, has an interesting defense mechanism in the wild—it wedges itself between rocks by crawling into crevices, taking in air, and then inflating its body.

GEORGE PISANI

The Green Iguana, *Iguana iguana*, is native to Central and South America, but there now are a number of introduced populations in the United States, in Florida and Hawaii. Such introduced animals are usually referred to as "alien" species. Photo by Isabelle Francais.

W. P. MARA

Unless you're serious about breeding Green Iguanas, *Iguana iguana*, it is best to purchase your specimens when they are very young. Raising any of the iguanids from their first year can be a lot of fun.

# TAXONOMY AND NATURAL HISTORY

Iguanids are lizards. Theoretically, all species of lizards in the family Iguanidae could be called "iguanas," but the word *iguana* is more normally reserved for a few of the larger species, most of which have a conspicuous crest along the back that may be particularly obvious in the males. A general term for any individual in the family is simply "iguanid." The best known and most popular "pet" iguanid is undoubtedly the Green Iguana, *Iguana iguana*. Within the confines of this book, I will be using the term "iguanid" to refer to any and all members of the family Iguanidae (see the end of this chapter for listing of genera contained therein), and individual species will of course be referred to by their individual names, both Latin and, where possible, common.

## CLASSIFICATION OF REPTILES

To get the story of the iguanids into perspective, it is necessary to start at the beginning. First we must see how they are classified in the animal kingdom, then we will discuss how they got to be where they are.

Lizards are reptiles and reptiles are animals. Reptiles are also vertebrates, or, animals with a backbone. Other vertebrates include fish, amphibians, birds, and mammals. Reptiles all have certain things in common, and a few things that no other vertebrates have. For example, all reptiles have a scaly skin in one form or another and all have

The Latin name of the Galapagos Land Iguana, which is *Conolophus subcristatus*, has an interesting etymological history—the genus, *Conolophus*, means "conical keel" and refers to the shape of the dorsal spines—they are cone-shaped rather than flattened, as they are with most other iguanids.

R. G. SPRACKLAND

lungs. Now, you may say fish have a scaly skin, but they do not have lungs! Other vertebrates, like amphibians, birds, and mammals may have lungs, but they have a smooth skin, feathers, or hair, instead of scales, so from these few small points we can already see how unique a reptile is.

The reptiles all share a large class called the "Reptilia." This class contains four groups of reptiles called orders, and each order contains groups of reptiles that have things in common, these most often being referred to as "families." There is an order for crocodiles, caimans, and alligators (Crocodylia), an order for turtles and tortoises (Chelonia), an order for the tuataras (Rhynchocephalia—the tuataras are primitive lizard-like reptiles from New Zealand that have several unique characteristics which place them in an order of their own. For many years there was only one tuatara species, but now it is generally believed that there are two) and, of course, an order for lizards

**Facing Page:** The spiny-tailed iguanas, genus *Ctenosaura*, were first described by Wiegmann in 1828. There are currently about ten species in the genus, all native to middle America. Specimen shown is a *Ctenosaura palearis*. Photo by R. D. Bartlett.

and snakes (Squamata). Lizards and snakes are lumped in a single order because they have so many characteristics in common even though they look quite different (in most cases—however, there are some legless lizards, for example, and a further suborder, Amphisbaenia, that help add to the confusion), but there are enough differences between lizards and snakes to make taxonomists (zoologists who classify living things scientifically) want to place each into separate suborders. Thus the snakes are put in the suborder Serpentes and lizards in the suborder Sauria.

WILLIAM B. ALLEN, JR.

Marine Iguanas, *Amblyrhynchus cristatus*, are among the most "relaxed" of the iguanids in regards to human interaction. People who have traveled to their native land report that you can literally walk right up and touch specimens on the nose.

## HISTORY OF THE CLASSIFICATION SYSTEM

It was the Swedish botanist Linnaeus (1707-1788) who more or less started off all this classification business, at least in relation to the system we are familiar with today. He saw the need to devise a logical system of classification in order to stamp out all the confusion arising from multi-lingual scientists of varied nations working on similar projects. Linnaeus thus took on the mammoth task of naming all of the then-known species of plants and animals through a system of "binomial nomenclature" that could be used internationally. In this system (which he published in his *Systema Naturae*), each species was given two Latin names (or names which have been "latinized," which are also commonly referred to as *scientific* names). The first name was the generic name (or name of the genus), while the second is the specific name (which identified an individual species within the genus). Latin names are international, so whatever a zoologist's native language is, he or she will still understand what animal is being referred to when they come across its Latin name.

The system of binomial nomenclature devised by Linnaeus is still used, but in a vastly superior form to the pioneer system because our knowledge of relationships has increased so much over the years. Publishing the description of newly discovered animal species is a strictly regulated procedure, governed by the International Code of Zoological Nomenclature. An international committee convenes at regular intervals to make decisions on whether or not a new species has been correctly named and to consider proposals for the changing of existing names brought about by reclassification in the light of new knowledge.

The application of a clean-cut binomen to a species is not without problems, however, and in some cases it is necessary to add a third name, making a trinomen. This is used when geographical groups of a species show certain differences but are not sufficiently different to be considered their own species. Such

groups of animals are known as subspecies, and while many lizards are regarded just as species (with a binomial), some may have quite a large number of subspecies. When a species is relegated to subspecific rank, the first (original) species

Spiny-tailed iguanas are not commonly seen in the hobby, but, in the right places, they may be seen in food markets! They are often hunted in their natural habitats and killed for their meat. Specimen shown is a *Ctenosaura quinquecarinatus*. Photo by R. D. Bartlett.

described has its specific name simply repeated, while further subspecies are given new names.

To illustrate the point, let's take a look at two North American iguanids:

The Spinytail Iguana (of Mexico and introduced into southern Texas

and southern Florida) is simply considered a monotypic species (one with no subspecies) and thus has the binomial *Ctenosaura pectinata*. Conversely, the Common Chuckwalla, *Sauromalus obesus*, is considered to have four subspecies, three of which occur in the USA: *Sauromalus obesus obesus* (Western Chuckwalla), *Sauromalus obesus multiforaminatus* (Glen Canyon Chuckwalla), and *Sauromalus obesus tumidus* (Arizona Chuckwalla).

Binomials and trinomials are written in italic or underlined script to avoid confusion with common names or the text in which they are cited. When it is necessary to use the binomials or trinomials several times in a given text, abbreviation is accepted as long as the name has been written once in full. *Ctenosaura pectinata*, for example, can be reduced to *C. pectinata*, and *Sauromalus obesus obesus* can be reduced to *S. o. obesus*.

### EVOLUTION OF THE IGUANIDS

In order to better understand the position of our modern iguanids in zoological classification, it is desirable to have a basic knowledge of their evolution.

It is generally accepted that all of the higher vertebrates evolved from various advanced fishes which themselves had evolved from non-vertebrates via more primitive fish-like ancestors. For millions of years, the only life on earth was aquatic until certain plants and invertebrates invaded the relatively hostile land environment.

During the Devonian Period, about

380 million years ago, the first fishes started to creep out of the water and onto the land. These lobe-finned fishes (so-named due to the tough, limb-like character of their fins), were typified by members of the genus *Eusthenopteron*, that had already developed primitive lungs to enable respiration out of the water and the ability to travel from one water source to another. Such fishes led directly to the first amphibians, which developed over a period of about 35 million years. The first amphibians were still probably fish-like in appearance but the limb-like fins had developed into pairs of arms and legs, each with five fingers or five toes respectively. Members of the genus *Ichthyostega* were typical examples of these primitive amphibians. They had relatively longer snouts than their fishy ancestors, allowing for a more highly developed sense of smell.

Many species of the amphibians that we are familiar with today developed during the Carboniferous Period, which followed the Devonian. Some of these became more terrestrial than others and exploited the opportunity to feed on the invertebrate prey that already lived on the land. After a time, many only needed to return to water for the purpose of reproducing though they always required reasonably high humidity in order to avoid desiccation. Therefore, they were not likely to wander far from permanent water.

To gain further benefit from terrestrial life, it was necessary for these amphibians to evolve better means of retaining moisture within the body. A major development was another protective layer of skin, which eventually developed into the typical reptilian scales. Reproduction remained a problem, however,

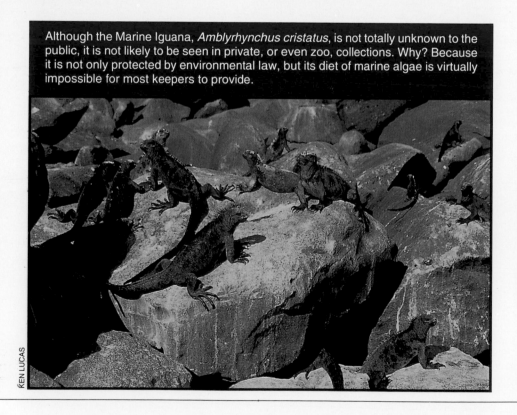

Although the Marine Iguana, *Amblyrhynchus cristatus*, is not totally unknown to the public, it is not likely to be seen in private, or even zoo, collections. Why? Because it is not only protected by environmental law, but its diet of marine algae is virtually impossible for most keepers to provide.

KEN LUCAS

K. H. SWITAK

Lizards and snakes were, at one time, only one group, but then they broke off into their respective subgroups (listed officially as suborders) sometime during the Jurassic Period. One appealing aspect of the Iguanidae is the dinosaur-like appearance of most of its members. Lizard shown is Lewis's Grand Cayman Island Iguana, *Cyclura nubila lewisi*.

because a means of preventing desiccation in eggs laid on land was needed. Unlike the amphibians, which had to return to water in order to lay their eggs (as most modern amphibians still do), the emerging reptiles found a means of reproducing on land—sometimes a considerable distance from water. This phenomenon became possible through the development of internal fertilization and the cleidoic egg (an egg with a thick, protective, and water-conserving shell). These eggs could be concealed from predators to some degree by being buried below the surface or hidden among dense vegetation. The eggs were large-yolked, and the embryos could develop to a reasonably advanced state inside the egg, thus avoiding the vulnerable free-larval stage of the amphibians. Enclosed in a sort of sac called the amniotic membrane, the embryo grew in the water-like contents, receiving oxygen through the membrane walls and disposing of carbon dioxide by means of the allantois, a further membrane. Another membrane, the chorion, enclosed the whole contents, just inside the tough, leathery, outer shell.

The reptiles became so successful on the land that they soon (in geological terms) ruled the earth. They developed many diverse forms and more efficient ways of preying on invertebrates or on each other. No herbivorous reptiles had yet developed during the early Permian Period so it was a tremendously

ANITA MALHOTRA

Many Green Iguana, *Iguana iguana*, enthusiasts are unaware that there is another species in the genus *Iguana*. It is *Iguana delicatissima*, known as the Antillean Iguana, and can only be found on a few Caribbean Islands. One of the features that delineates it from the Green Iguana is the fact that it has no enlarged subtympanic scale.

MICHAEL CARDWELL

Most members of the genus *Cyclura* are herbivorous, meaning they feed primarily on plant matter. Although such a diet would be fairly easy for the average keeper to provide, the Rhinoceros Iguanas are environmentally protected and thus can't be privately kept in the first place.

competitive time. Various adaptations for gripping, tearing, and chewing, as well as for means of protection, had to be developed. Limbs lengthened and grew under the body rather than the sides, thus allowing greater speed and stamina. Herbivores developed to take advantage of the prolific plant life. Para-mammals and true mammals also began to evolve during this period, as did the dinosaurs which kept all other forms of life oppressed for the next 140 million years (through to the end of the Cretaceous). The main ancestors of the crocodilians developed during this period and have changed very little from then until now. The Rhynchocephalians also developed at this time, but the only surviving members of this group today are the two species of Tuatara, *Sphenodon punctatus*, and the Brother Island Tuatara, *Sphenodon guentheri*, both of New Zealand. The Chelonia (the turtles and tortoises) probably started as a separate group around the late Permian and were at their most prolific during the Jurassic and Cretaceous periods. In several respects they can be regarded as the most primitive of the living reptiles.

Today's snakes and lizards could have arisen from groups of Rhynchosauria, the same ancestors

Found from southern Nevada south to both northern Sinaloa and all throughout Baja California, the Desert Iguana, *Dipsosaurus dorsalis*, can be tough to maintain in captivity since many specimens require a daytime temperature of over 100°F/38°C. Native to sandy habitats, it mainly is a herbivorous animal, only occasionally taking small insects and carrion. Photo by R. D. Bartlett.

of the tuataras. Some believe they split from the line into their two respective suborders during the Jurassic Period. The oldest ancestors of our modern lizards are seen in fossils from the late Jurassic, about 200 million years ago. (Interestingly, the first fossil bird ancestors appeared at about the same time.) Snakes pose a great evolutionary problem, and very little is known about their early history. They possibly arose from the lizard line during the Cretaceous Period at the same time the ancestors of our iguanids were appearing (about 110 million years ago). Due to the delicate structure of the bones of small lizards and snakes, fossil study material is extremely sparse. The oldest known fossils that are undoubtedly iguanids come from the Oligocene Period (about 35 million years ago) of North America, but it can be said that the ancestors of our modern iguanids were developing well before this time and many have probably remained relatively unchanged.

It is most probable that the early ancestors of the Iguanidae arose in North America. The headquarters of today's iguanids is undoubtedly the Americas although there are some remnant populations in Madagascar and on the Fiji Islands—perhaps an indication of a more cosmopolitan

Perhaps the most obvious characteristic of the popular Green Iguana, *Iguana iguana*, is the large subtympanic scale, which in normal English means the scale "below the ear," and which can be seen quite clearly in this photo.

WILLIAM B. ALLEN, JR.

range in the past. One possible reason why iguanids became extinct in many parts of the world is because of intense competition from other lizard families, in particular the Old World agamids, who filled all of the climatic and topographic niches in Africa, Asia, and Australasia that were similar to those occupied by iguanids in the New World.

## MODERN IGUANID CLASSIFICATION

The family Iguanidae is the predominant group of lizards in the New World and there is a great range of sizes, shapes, and habits among the various genera and species. The question as to exactly which genera make up this family has been given a number of different answers in recent years, but in this particular book the guidelines that will be followed are those given in an article entitled "The Name Game: Goodbye to Iguanids

and Agamids" in the December 1991 issue of the magazine *Tropical Fish Hobbyist*. The conclusions presented by the author are based on those made in a 65-page scientific paper by noted herpetologists Darrel Frost and Richard Etheridge entitled "A phylogenetic analysis and taxonomy of iguanian lizards (Reptilia: Squamata)" (University of Kansas Museum of Natural History, *Miscellaneous Publication*: 81)."

In short, the family Iguanidae, which previously contained over 50 genera (and over 700 species), is now confined to only these eight genera: *Amblyrhynchus* (Marine Iguanas), *Brachylophus* (Fiji Iguanas), *Conolophus* (Galapagos Land Iguanas), *Ctenosaura* (Black Iguanas), *Cyclura* (Rhinoceros Iguana), *Dipsosaurus* (Desert Iguanas), *Iguana* (the Green and Antillean Iguanas), and *Sauromalus* (Chuckwallas).

Although at one time the family Iguanidae contained at least 50 genera, it has now been trimmed down to having only eight—*Amblyrhynchus, Brachylophus, Conolophus, Ctenosaura, Cyclura, Dipsosaurus, Iguana,* and *Sauromalus.* The lizard shown is a Desert Iguana, *Dipsosaurus dorsalis.*

K. H. SWITAK

One of the most attractive of all iguanids is the Fiji Island Iguana, *Brachylophus fasciatus*. Although reportedly an excellent captive, the Fiji Island Iguana is heavily protected by environmental law and cannot be kept by private individuals. Photo by R. D. Bartlett.

Housing most iguanids is not a difficult undertaking as long as you accept the fact that many of them will grow to a large size and should thus be allowed to roam freely once in awhile. These two little Green Iguanas, *Iguana iguana*, for example, will grow to about five or six feet if properly cared for. Photo by Isabelle Francais.

# HOUSING

A cage in which herptiles are kept is usually called a *terrarium* (although many hobbyists refer to it as a *vivarium*). A terrarium should be of sufficient size for the animals to be both comfortable and supplied with the necessary life-support systems (heating, lighting, humidity, ventilation, etc.) required by the species being kept. Additionally, the enclosure should be easy to clean and have an aesthetically pleasing appearance. Finally, it must of course be escape-proof!

enjoyable to experiment with various items obtained from secondhand or do-it-yourself stores.

## TYPICAL TANKS

At one time, simple aquarium tanks were used to house many pet species. For small iguanids or the juveniles of larger species, they are ideal, especially if you want to maintain a high humidity. You must ensure that there is adequate ventilation, bearing in mind that air usually enters a tank only at the top.

PHOTO COURTESY OF CREATIVE SUPRIZES

Placing a piece of scenic sheeting on the back of a lizard's tank will not only create an illusion of depth, but also add a nice visual touch to any arrangement.

The terrarium shape is relatively unimportant. However, it is wise to use fairly tall cages for arboreal species of iguanids and fairly shallow ones for terrestrial types. It is now possible to buy ready-made terraria complete with all their life-support systems, but many enthusiasts still prefer to make their own. They may be constructed from many different types of material, and it can be very

With the help of silicone rubber sealant, it is possible to construct glass terrariums in many shapes and sizes, and by using a combination of glass and acrylic materials, you can have ventilation holes drilled in the sides or back (it is easy to drill holes in acrylic sheeting). Glass is extremely good for making a setup in which part of the floor is to be a permanent water feature. The lid for a glass terrarium preferably should be made of plywood or plastic and have wire mesh-covered holes through which the heating and lighting apparatus can function.

Timber can be used to construct a terrarium but the wood must have a few coats of varnish or non-toxic paint or it will quickly deteriorate in damp situations. A simple terrarium for smaller species consisting of a plywood box with a framed glass front drilled through the ends of the cage about one-third the distance from the base, and further holes should be drilled through the top to allow for convection. Instead of individual holes, you may want to cut out a large square and cover the opening with fine mesh. Narrow wooden beading may be framed around the edges of the mesh to give a neat effect. A sliding metal, plastic, or wooden tray can be fitted in the base

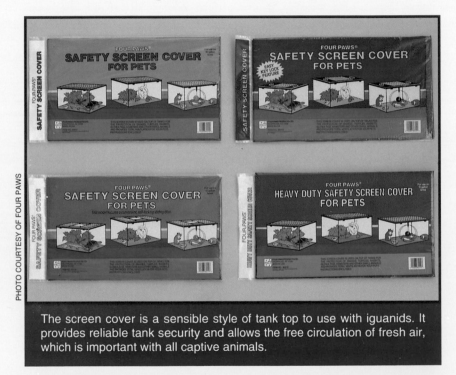

PHOTO COURTESY OF FOUR PAWS

The screen cover is a sensible style of tank top to use with iguanids. It provides reliable tank security and allows the free circulation of fresh air, which is important with all captive animals.

is easy to make. Using 10 mm/½ in plywood, the top, bottom, and ends are simply tacked and glued together.

A glass viewing panel may be slid into grooves on the top and bottom or in the sides. Alternatively, you may wish to mount the glass in a wooden frame, which can then be attached to the front of the cage with hinges (beware, though, that since some iguanids can grow quite large, the possibility of one of them smashing through a glass pane is very real). Groups of ventilation holes should be of the box to hold the substrate for easier cleaning.

For larger specimens you will naturally need a much larger cage. Though you can make such a cage from timber, I have seen many fine terrariums manufactured from such things as old cabinets or chests. You may be able to get some old aluminum or timber-framed windows from a demolition yard and incorporate these into your terrarium. The minimum dimensions for, say, a pair of adult Green

Many keepers like to use wood products in conjunction with their iguanid setups, but it should be pointed out that wood is very difficult to clean once it gets soiled; most items probably will have to be thrown out and replaced. Lizard shown is a Green Iguana, *Iguana iguana*. Photo by Jim Merli.

Iguanas or similar should be 180 cm wide x 180 cm high x 90 cm deep (approximately 6ft x 6 ft x 3 ft).

## THE PERMANENT TERRARIUM

A permanent terrarium built into a part of the house or apartment can be an incredibly attractive feature; it can be a focal point in the den, living room, hall, or conservatory. Such a terrarium could be made in an alcove, or it could be free-standing. Really substantial terrariums, especially suitable for large species like the Green or Rhinoceros Iguanas, can be built with concrete blocks or bricks and could include a permanent, drainable, concrete pool and artificial cliff-faces with ledges and keeper-accessible hiding caves. Where smaller species are being kept, you can include pockets among the rockwork, nicely arranged with potted plants. A visit to a zoo that has a reptile house will no doubt give you several ideas as well.

A word of warning—before commencing any major construction, be sure you are not violating any building regulations. It may also be a good idea to get professional advice before introducing weighty structures

If you have the land space, you could always provide your larger iguanid pets with a penned-in area replete with all the natural components that go with it. This large Galapagos Land Iguana, *Conolophus subcristatus*, for example, would much prefer the area it's already lying in rather than be stuck in a large glass aquarium (although this species isn't allowed to be privately kept in the first place).

R. WALLACE

R. WALLACE

Some iguanids, whether they can be legally kept or not, simply shouldn't be, for obvious reasons. This Marine Iguana, *Amblyrhynchus cristatus*, for example, could only be happy if it was provided with a bunch of large rocks and a good-sized body of salt water; neither of these items would be easy for a keeper to furnish.

into your home. More than once a hobbyist has built a heavy terrarium setup on an upper floor only to have it come crashing down onto the floor below a short time later.

### OUTDOOR ENCLOSURES

If you happen to live in an area where wild iguanids of one sort or another occur, or if you live in an area where they do not occur but the climate is still suitable, you may want to consider keeping them in an outdoor enclosure. Iguanids will benefit enormously from the fresh air and sunlight, and many will be able to live almost natural lives in the right setting, even foraging for much of their own food (although it's not a good idea to depend on this completely). They will also be able to behave territorially and are thus more likely to breed, though the ensuing eggs will still have to be removed for artificial incubation.

A typical outdoor enclosure usually consists of a central mound surrounded by a secure wall. The size of the enclosure will depend on the amount of available space you have, what you can afford in building materials, and the number and size of the iguanids you wish to keep. Use an area that receives as much

R. D. BARTLETT

If you decide to keep a larger iguanid pet outside, remember that they are skilled climbers. The walls of the pen should not only be high, but have a deterrent element along the top, such as an inward slope. Lizard shown is a Fiji Island Iguana, *Brachylophus fasciatus.*

sunlight as possible—many keepers assure this by having a large part of the mound's slope facing south. When digging the foundation of the wall, be sure to bury it at least 50 cm/20 in down to prevent the inmates from digging their way to freedom. One helpful tip: use the earth removed for the foundations to start the central mound.

For most smaller iguanids (*Sauromalus* spp. for example), the height of the wall need not be more than 120 cm/4 ft. However, it must be considerably higher for the larger species (up to 180 to 210 cm/6 or 7 ft). The wall can be built with bricks or concrete blocks and then smoothed off with a fine cement. To prevent the more agile specimens from escaping, an inward-slope of at least 30 cm/12 in should run along the wall's top. Also, leave a space of about 120 cm/4 ft between the wall and the start of the central mound so as to discourage your captives from trying to jump from the top of the mound to the top of the wall. This space can take the form of a concrete-based moat containing water or it can be covered with clean gravel free of plants and debris.

A pond, waterfall, stream, etc. in your enclosure will make an attractive feature. The central mound can be tastefully decorated with rocks and logs and planted with various plants and a few shrubs. Flowering plants will attract flying insects, which will be a welcome addition to the menu. It is also wise to provide a few sandy, plant-free areas where breeder specimens can burrow and lay their eggs.

## GREENHOUSE ACCOMMODATIONS

The best of both worlds can be achieved with a heated greenhouse. Such a setup will provide a nice free-range accommodation for sub-tropical and tropical species and is the nearest compromise to an outdoor enclosure you can have in a temperate climate. The main disadvantage is the expense of creating and maintaining the right conditions in such a large volume of space, but if you can afford to overcome this you will not regret it. A miniature rain forest of sorts can be created, and high levels of humidity can be maintained by using sprinklers, heated pools, and waterfalls (remember, though, that iguanids will not do well if the humidity is *too* high). Heat lamps should be placed in several positions, giving your pets a choice of both warm and cool basking sites. Remember also to keep the lamps a good distance away from water. The ambient temperature should not fall below 18°C/65°F at night, and care should be taken to ensure that overheating does not occur on summer days. A keeper should purchase one of the many different thermostats available from hardware stores, home improvement centers, etc. to ensure steady and correct

All iguanids need full-spectrum lighting in order to survive. In short, artificial full-spectrum light replicates that given off by the sun, which provides lizards with vitamin D3. Lizard shown is a Green Iguana, *Iguana iguana*.

W. P. MARA

temperatures. Windows and ventilation holes should be covered with wire mesh to prevent escapes, and pipes and other heating apparatus should be boxed or caged to prevent the animal from burning themselves.

### DECORATIONS AND FURNISHINGS

Your pets's terrarium(s) will require various furnishings that are both functional and decorative. Although it is possible to keep and breed some iguanids in almost "clinical" conditions (a sheet of absorbent varieties. Coarse sand can be used for a desert-type terrarium, while a mixture of peat, sand, and loam can be used in a woodland-type terrarium. For larger species, it is best to use aquarium gravel (be sure to wash it thoroughly beforehand), which can be obtained in various shapes, sizes, and colors. Avoid finer sand because it tends to cake between a reptile's scales.

Whatever substrate material you end up using, remember that it must be removed and washed or disposed of and replaced at regular intervals;

PHOTO COURTESY OF DURA PRO

The "Lizard Loft" is a sensible product for keepers who need to provide their iguanids with something to climb and rest upon. Lizard lofts are relatively inexpensive and can be used with most any glass aquarium.

paper, a water dish, and a hiding box), most enthusiasts seem to want a terrarium that is visually satisfying as well as practical (although the aforementioned clinical setup can be of immense convenience when cleaning time comes around).

### Floor Coverings

Substrate material comes in many and the larger the species, the more often this must be done.

### Rocks

Rocks of all kinds are not only decorative in a terrarium, but also serve as functional basking sites and, if properly configured, hiding places. You can get suitable rocks at your local pet store or garden center, but some people like to go out and find their own (although if you decide to do this, don't forget to obtain permission from whoever owns the land you're searching on). Always ensure that the rocks are placed firmly so they don't topple down and injure one of your pets. When large piles of rocks are used, especially in the construction of a hiding spot, it is best to cement them together rather than run the risk of having them collapse and, again, hurt one of the animals.

### Tree Branches and Logs

Strong tree branches are very important for arboreal species. It is more practical to use a dead tree branch and grow a creeping house plant on it rather than grow a tree or shrub. For the larger herbivorous iguanids, growing any plants at all will be a waste of time because they will simply eat them. Try and select branches with interesting shapes; gnarled and twisted limbs are always attractive to look at. Driftwood collected from the seashore or from river banks is often visually appealing as it will have been weathered by the sand, sun, and water. All wood should be thoroughly scrubbed, rinsed, and dried before being used, and then carefully cleaned again every time it is defecated on. In fact, a piece of decorative wood will reach a point where it will have to be discarded since cleanliness will

PHOTO COURTESY OF FOUR PAWS

Four Paws Terrarium Linings are fully washable and mildew-resistant. The thick fibers of the linings provides a happy and healthy environment for small animals.

simply not be guaranteeable anymore. You may want to immerse some logs in a solution of bleach for a day or two to give it a more weathered appearance, but don't forget to rinse it thoroughly (by soaking it repeatedly in cold water) before use to remove the excess bleach. Larger logs and branches should be securely fixed in position to ensure that they cannot fall and injure the inmates. Using screws, wire, and a little creative thought, you can accomplish this easily enough.

### Plants

Healthy plants in an iguanid's setup undoubtedly provide a lovely visual touch (although again, beware that largely herbivorous species will very likely eat these plants). Unless the enclosure is very large, however, it is futile to try and grow plants where large robust iguanids are being kept since the plants continually will be uprooted or flattened.

For smaller iguanids, a terrarium may be attractively planted. Make sure you select plant species compatible to the type of environment contained therein. Many house plants are suitable and it will be useful to study a good book on houseplant culture to aid in your selection. Plants are best left in pots and concealed behind rocks or in special cavities in logs or rockwork. It is then easy to remove and replace the plants in case they get "sick." It is advisable to have spare potted plants in similar-sized pots so that they can be exchanged at, say, monthly intervals or at cleaning time. The plant which has suffered the rigors of terrarium life can then be given a period of rest and recuperation in a greenhouse or on a window-ledge until its partner requires similar aid.

### LIFE-SUPPORT SYSTEMS

Certain *natural* life-support aids are not available for the indoor terrarium, so the keeper must

can, however, still move in and out of warm or cool places whenever they wish, so they can control that temperature to some degree (by basking directly in the sun or by absorbing heat from sun-warmed soil, rocks, or other items). In cooler climates, during times when the sun is not warm enough to supply optimum temperatures, iguanids will hibernate until the preferred warmth returns.

Using natural sunlight through terrarium glass poses problems of overheating, though this can be

PHOTO COURTESY OF FOUR PAWS

There are a great number of products designed to aid a keeper with the provision of heat. Check your local pet shop to find which item best suits the needs of both you and your pets.

provide artificial systems to compensate. Such aids include heating, lighting, humidity, and ventilation. For the first three, the amounts needed will vary from species to species, but the fourth, ventilation, is important for any and all lizards.

### HEATING

Iguanids are, as many readers are no doubt already aware, cold-blooded, or, to use a more technical term, *poikilothermic*. This means their body temperature is controlled by the temperature of the environment that immediately surrounds them. They

overcome in the summer by using insect screening or mesh for the tank top so as to allow the warm air to rise up and out rather than be trapped inside.

You must, of course, be aware of the particular temperatures required by each individual species and remember that most iguanids, apart from those inhabiting lowland equatorial areas, require a fairly substantial reduction in temperature at night (around 8 to 10°C/46 to 50°F). In your home, this can be accomplished by simply switching off the heat source and allowing the terrarium to cool to room temperature (provided, of course, you live in an area where "room temperature" is indeed notably cooler during the night hours).

### Incandescent Light Bulbs

Ordinary household incandescent light bulbs had long been used as the sole source of heating and lighting in the home terrarium, but then it was discovered that the spectral quality of light emitted was insufficient for iguanids. However, incandescent bulbs should not be ignored completely because they are inexpensive, emit a fair amount of heat, and will supply adequate supplementary light. The size of the terrarium will dictate what size bulb(s) to use. By experimenting with various bulb wattages and a thermometer, the correct type of bulb to use will be revealed. A bulb may be concealed inside a flower pot or metal canister and controlled by a thermostat so that a constant, minimum background temperature is maintained.

### Heat Lamps

Various kinds of lamps are available that produce radiant heat. The type used in poultry brooders or piggeries can be directed at iguanid basking areas. Set up the lamp at one end of the tank so you'll have a temperature gradation between that end and the other. The iguanids will then be able to choose which area they wish to bask in. Ceramic heating bulbs are also available. These are sometimes referred to as a "black lights," and emit heat but no light. These are useful for maintaining background heat at night.

### Cable Heaters and Pads

Utilized by horticulturists in their propagating boxes, cable heaters and heating pads also can be used for

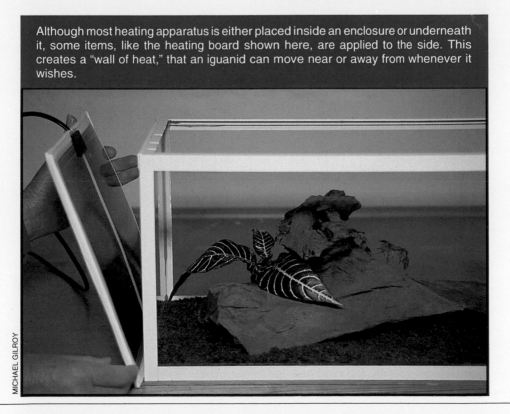

Although most heating apparatus is either placed inside an enclosure or underneath it, some items, like the heating board shown here, are applied to the side. This creates a "wall of heat," that an iguanid can move near or away from whenever it wishes.

MICHAEL GILROY

If you have provided your iguanids with a large, permanent water body, you can heat that water body quite easily by using a fully submersible heater. Such heaters come in a variety of sizes and wattages and can be found at most pet shops. Photo courtesy of Hagen.

warming parts of the tank floor. Generally inexpensive, they can be purchased at a number of places, including pet and plant shops.

### Aquarium Heaters

Aquarium heaters are useful for maintaining both warmth and humidity in a terrarium, and are virtually indispensable in a tropical rainforest setup. Placed in a glass or ceramic water vessel, an aquarium heater will keep the water in the vessel warm, and the air in the tank warm and humid. By using an airstone attached to an aerator pump along with an aquarium heater (by submerging the "airstone" into the same water body), you can increase

humidity even further, provide additional ventilation, and, to a small degree, help keep the water fresh.

### LIGHTING

Natural sunlight, or a good substitute, is essential for the health of all iguanids. The most important elements of sunlight, as far as iguanids are concerned, are the ultra-violet rays that catalyze the manufacture of vitamin D3. This vitamin helps control the actions of calcium and phosphorus in the body. Without it, various health problems will most assuredly ensue. If it is possible for you to supply your iguanids with natural sunlight, then by all means do so. Keep in mind that natural sunlight shining through glass is not beneficial to iguanids because the ultra-violet rays are filtered out. In temperate areas, during certain times of the

It is always a good idea to closely monitor the ambient temperature of your iguanids, so it is advised that you invest in a reliable thermometer.

year, a terrarium cannot be placed outside and thus some form of alternative lighting must be provided. Special fluorescent tubes which emit a preponderance of light from the "blue" end of the spectrum will provide sufficient ultra-violet light for your iguanids. Be aware, though, that too much ultra-violet light can be more damaging than too little. Research into suitable light sources for the captive keeping of flora and

**HUMIDITY**

Iguanids that are native to rainforest areas will require an atmosphere in captivity that is more or less humid all the time, while species from other regions will require seasonal increases in humidity. The provision of high intense amount of heat as well, so keep them high above both the plants and the animals.

Since proper lighting is essential with iguanids, there are a number of bulbs that will provide you with the quality of light needed. Most of these bulbs cost a little more than ordinary fluorescents, but they are well worth it.

fauna is continuing, and information on the subject can be garnered if the hobbyist is willing to do a little of their own research. Books like this and others can be purchased, or at the very least ordered, through your local pet store or through any number of distributors who advertise in national magazines, journals, and club newsletters.

In darker indoor situations where high intensity lighting is required, quartz-halogen lamps can be considered. These lamps are particularly useful in the promotion of lush plant growth, but keep in mind that they also emit a fairly

humidity in the terrarium is quite easy as there are a number of methods at the keeper's disposal. A submersible aquarium heater can be placed in a water dish or a separate jar of water that has been filled high enough so the heater will not be damaged. As I mentioned earlier, an aerator used in the water will further increase the humidity and air temperature and thus is ideal for use in a tropical rainforest setup. One method of maintaining humidity in a planted terrarium is to simply spray-mist it, but this must be done two or three times a day. If that is not practical for you, you can always resort to a "drip system," in which a drip of water is released at regular intervals onto rocks or foliage. This can be achieved with a hospital intravenous drip bag filled with water and the delivery tube regulator adjusted to allow only very slow drippage. Similar drip systems can be made using a large soft drink or

for disease organisms to thrive and multiply. Additionally, a badly ventilated terrarium will develop a number of unpleasant growths and as a consequence become very unpleasant-smelling. Ensure, therefore, that there is a regular, free-flowing air exchange in the terrarium, but be careful not allow

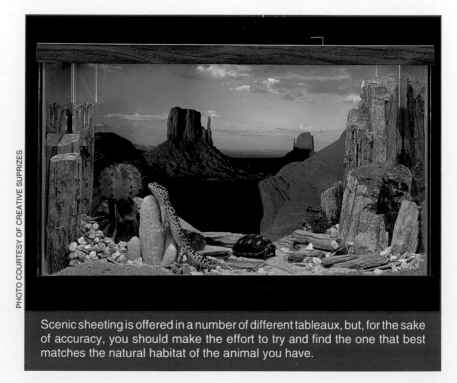

PHOTO COURTESY OF CREATIVE SUPRIZES

Scenic sheeting is offered in a number of different tableaux, but, for the sake of accuracy, you should make the effort to try and find the one that best matches the natural habitat of the animal you have.

milk container filled with water, a narrow tube (like the kind used with fishtank filters), and a clamp. The container is placed higher than the terrarium top and the water is run through the tube. The tightness of the clamp will control the amount of drippage.

**VENTILATION**

In a confine as cramped as even the largest terrarium can be, adequate ventilation is very important. A lack of it will lead to a build up of stagnant air resulting in an excess of carbon dioxide. This in turn will provide favorable conditions

cold drafts. In most cases, the keeper need not do much more than drill some holes through the top and sides of the terrarium (although with glass tanks, of course, this will not be the case). Any warmth generated by a heating apparatus will cause convection currents, the warm air leaving through the top and fresh air replacing it through the side vents.

An aquarium aerator operated from a small air pump can be used to supply extra ventilation. If low humidity is required, the aerator should not be put in water. When a terrarium is situated in a place where people gather frequently, like a living room for example, it is recommended that the air inlet is placed outside the room. This is also applicable to rooms where heavy smokers are present. In colder conditions, the air tube can be laid near an underfloor heater or radiator so the chill is removed before the air enters the terrarium.

**SAFETY PRECAUTIONS**

Since heating and lighting apparatus in a terrarium will be operated by electricity, you must take adequate safety precautions to avoid electrical accidents. Unless you are an adept electrician, only use equipment which has passed safety standards, and then only use it to the manufacturer's explicit instructions. If in doubt, employ a qualified electrician to do your wiring and installing for you. Also, be sure to turn off all electrical components when you are working in and around your terrarium. Never forget: electricity and water are a perilous combination.

Since most iguanids are fairly active creatures, you should always keep safety precautions in mind. There has been more than one case of a young iguanid being injured because its keeper did not efficiently assess the animal's surroundings in regards to safety. Lizard shown is a young Green Iguana, *Iguana iguana*.

W. P. MARA

K. H. SWITAK

Ouch! No, eating the bud from this cactus does not hurt this Galapagos Land Iguana, *Conolophus subcristatus*; in fact, cactus buds and fruits are a regular part of their diet.

# FEEDING

The nutritional requirements of captive reptiles have, until recently, been poorly understood. What was known in the past was mainly speculative, based on what each particular species was known (or thought) to eat in the wild coupled with what was known about the nutritional requirements of domestic or agricultural animals. Research into the latter is, of course, a matter of economic necessity while research into the nutrition of reptiles is more "incidental."

However, an increase in the popularity of iguanids and other reptiles over the past few decades has led to an increase in the research of their nutrition as well. This research, coupled with the knowledge previously accumulated over the years by amateur and professional herpetologists, has led to the wonderful situation we have today, where no captive iguanid needs to be nutritionally deficient in any way whatsoever.

Every animal must receive a balanced diet if it is to enjoy optimum health, and such a diet consists of a number of primary nutritional elements taken in appropriate amounts. These elements are discussed here.

Since iguanid lizards are so popular, a number of companies have begun producing foods specially designed to fulfill the nutritional needs of these animals. Check your local pet shop to see which types they carry. Photo courtesy of Pretty Pets.

## PRIMARY NUTRIENTS

* Proteins: for the growth, repair, and replacement of body tissues as well as many other biological functions. Proteins are in both animal and vegetable material but are most readily available in the former.

* Carbohydrates: for immediate energy requirements. Sugars and starches, for example, are obtained primarily in vegetable matter.

* Fats: for stored energy requirements, insulation, and shock absorption. Occur both as animal fats and plant oils.

"Pseudonutrients"

* Minerals (particularly calcium and phosphorus): for bone growth and repair, proper function of the cell membranes, and the buffering of body fluids. Also, trace elements such as iron, potassium, sodium, manganese, chlorine, and sulphur, all play their important roles. Minerals are contained in a variety of animal and vegetable materials.

* Vitamins (particularly, but not exclusively, vitamins A, B1, B2 complex, D3, and E): Vitamins have many functions. A deficiency of them (a condition known as avitaminosis) can result in many serious problems. Vitamins are present in virtually all normally prescribed iguanid foodstuffs.

W. P. MARA

As many experienced Green Iguana keepers already know, some Green Iguana specimens will eat just about anything! However, that doesn't mean you should *give* them just anything. Macaroni, for example, which seems quite appealing to this Green Iguana, has a great fat content. Go to the trouble of learning what should and shouldn't go into your pet's body before you start offering anything unorthodox.

W. P. MARA

In addition to the nutrients, fresh water must always be available. Although not considered a nutrient itself, water provides the medium through which all metabolic functions proceed.

In the wild, iguanid species acquire their foods in various ways and in various amounts, but it can be safely assumed that *what* they eat depends on what is naturally available. Remember that a species lives in the same habitat for thousands (maybe millions) of years, so there will be a very close ecological relationship between that animal and its food supply.

Data on what foods individual species eat in the wild is still sparse. We may see a wild iguanid catch a grasshopper, but this does not mean that grasshoppers are its sole food or even its main food. Analyzation of the feces of free-living reptiles often has given an indication as to what they eat. Unfortunately, the only sure way of analyzing the diet of a wild population is to capture large numbers of specimens and systematically examine their stomach contents over a number of seasons. This usually involves a lot of time and effort and occasionally endangers the health of the animals. It is often difficult, and in some instances practically impossible, to provide our captives with the exact type of foods they take naturally, but we are usually able to offer suitable substitutes. The secret of success here is not so much the quantity of foodstuffs, but the variety.

With regard to their feeding habits, iguanids can be can be split into three main groups:

* Carnivorous: feeding on living tissue, ranging from small invertebrates to larger vertebrates depending on the size of the animal. This encompasses the majority of iguanids.

* Herbivorous: feeding on plant material. One of the iguanids we are focusing on most sharply in this book, the Green Iguana, *Iguana iguana*, is primarily herbivorous.

* Omnivorous: feeding on a fairly equal mixture of plant material and living tissue.

Small Green Iguanas, *Iguana iguana*, can be fed much like dogs and cats—right from a bowl. Photo by Isabelle Francais.

These groups are far from being mutually exclusive. For example, a carnivore that swallows a whole prey animal will also be swallowing the contents of that animal's stomach, which may include a good amount of plant material. Conversely, a herbivore will consume a fair amount of the faunal life associated with the plant material it eats, like a Green Iguana eating a cricket that just happens to be crawling across the plant leaf it's chewing on.

**FOOD ITEMS**
Before deciding which species of iguanid you would like to keep, you should first ascertain whether or not you can provide a steady supply of

various foods for it. With some species this can be very difficult. Some horned lizards, like those in the genus *Phrynosoma*, for example (which, incidentally, is no longer considered a part of the family Iguanidae but rather is placed in its own family, Phrynosomatidae), feed almost exclusively on ants in the wild. Although some specimens may take other insects, it seems that in most cases ants are the only preferred food. Thus, it is not surprising that their physiology seems geared toward the need for this singular item. There is evidence that ants help maintain an optimum pH in the alimentary tract of these lizards. The feeding requirements of various iguanids are given with the species descriptions later in the text but some general ideas on the types of foods you can use for various species are given here.

## COLLECTED LIVEFOODS

While there are many types of livefoods that can be propagated in the home or purchased at regular intervals, the value of collecting foods in the wild cannot be overestimated. If you live in a highly developed city and do not have any transportation, collecting wild livefoods may be difficult, but still not impossible. Even in backyards, parks, railway embankments, and so forth, you will probably be able to find a few items. Also, the next time you take a weekend jaunt out to the country, spend an hour or so looking for livefoods there. A variety of wild-caught invertebrates and vertebrates will forestall the dangers of a monotonous diet.

One of the best methods of obtaining insects and spiders in the wild is by "foliage sweeping." You can do this by by passing a large, fine-

Chuckwallas, *Sauromalus obesus*, aren't particularly difficult to feed in captivity, but a keeper must remember their main diet—desert plants, not insects. Many a keeper has ended up with a dead Chuckwalla because they were unaware that "Chucks" are primarily herbivorous.

PAUL FREED

meshed net (a butterfly net is ideal) through the foliage of trees, shrubs, and tall grasses. Doing this in the warmer months will provide large quantities of beetles, bugs, caterpillars, grasshoppers, and spiders—all items that most carnivorous iguanids will eagerly accept.

Another method is to place a white sheet under a tree or shrub and vigorously shake the foliage. Although a few bugs may fall onto you and go down your shirt

found in a number of places. The soft, white bodies of these "white-ants" make them an excellent food for iguanids. You can transfer the termites into the terrarium by holding a piece of the termite nest in the tank and shaking it.

During the warmer parts of the

Hand-feeding young Green Iguanas, *Iguana iguana*, is not only a good way to get them eating, but also a good way to get them used to the company of humans. An iguanid lizard that has been hand-fed all its life will take its food more gently than those specimens that have not. Photo by Isabelle Francais.

(avoid this by wearing a broad-rimmed hat), many more will fall onto the sheet, and can then be easily collected. Place the captured insects in a jar or a plastic container for transport. And remember not to put too many insects into an iguanid's terrarium at any one time; allow the lizard(s) to consume a few at a time. If you have too many "extras" in a tank that is not completely secure, you will have escapees in the house.

One more way of obtaining livefoods is to search under rocks, rotten logs, and other ground debris. Damp areas will produce large numbers of springtails, beetles, woodlice (slaters), earthworms, slugs, snails, and so on. If you break open rotting timber you are likely to find grubs of many sorts. Termites can be

year, the flower garden is an ideal spot for collecting small insects. Small flies and tiny beetles (which are especially useful in the feeding of juvenile lizards) congregate among the flower petals. These can be collected using a "pooter," which is a glass or plastic bottle with two bungs and a glass tube passed through each. One of the tubes has a piece of rubber tubing about 15 cm/6 in long attached to it. One way insects can be caught is by placing the end of the rubber tube into the corolla of a flower and sucking sharply on the other tube with your mouth. The insects will be pulled through the long tube and fall into the bottle. A piece of cotton wadding placed loosely in the mouthpiece tube will stop you from accidentally getting a mouthful of bugs!

A very useful food item for small juvenile iguanids that is usually easy to obtain is the aphid (also known as the greenfly, blackfly, etc.). During the summer months, these tiny insects may be found in great numbers on the new green shoots of both domestic and wild plants. To feed aphids to your iguanids, simply break off an infested shoot and place it in the terrarium.

Nocturnal insects can be caught in quantity by way of something called a "light-trap." A floodlight, spotlight, or other strong light is directed onto a large, white surface (the side of a building, a white sheet, etc.), and the insects are attracted to the bright surface. They are then caught and placed in a container. There are quite a few lizards, including some iguanids, that feed on ants, and ants are a food item that can sometimes be difficult to obtain, particularly during the winter months in temperate zones.

Various fly species, in both larval and adult form, are suitable for carnivorous lizards. Houseflies, like *Musca*, *Fannia*, and others, are an excellent food for smaller iguanids while the larger green–and blue-bottles, such as *Lucilia* and *Calliphora*, for example, may be suitable for larger iguanid species. You can catch a variety of flies in a store-bought or homemade flytrap during the summer months. You make one by taking a 30-cm/12-in cubic framework and covering all of it, except for the base, with a fine mesh, such as insect-screening, muslin, or old net-curtain material. The framework is then mounted on a flat wooden board with a 5-cm/2-in hole in the center, and an inverted plastic funnel is placed over the hole. The trap is placed in a suitable spot (preferably well-away from your house), set on a platform about 5

cm/2 in from the ground with a fairly well-lit space beneath. A piece of strong-smelling meat or fish is then placed under the trap near the hole in the board, and soon numerous flies will be attracted to the bait. If you give the board an occasional tap, the flies will panic and make for the nearest source of light—through the funnel and into the trap. The flies can then be extracted by attaching a muslin sleeve to one side of the trap, through which you can pass a jar. When not in use, the sleeve can be knotted at the end. To reduce the incidence of escapees when adding the flies to the terrarium, place the jar containing the flies in the refrigerator for 10 minutes or so.

### Cultured Livefoods

There are quite a number of livefood items currently being cultured in captivity, most of which can be given to your carnivorous iguanid pets.

Mealworms are a good example of a popular cultured livefood. These are the larvae of the flour or grain beetle, *Tenebrio molitor*. These have long been cultivated as a food supply for captive insectivorous animals. While mealworms are known to be fairly nutritious, they do have their limitations and should be used only as a small part of a varied diet rather than a major part or, even worse, the only part. As far as the nutritional needs of iguanids are concerned, the main item mealworms are lacking is calcium. However, this can be compensated for quite easily by sprinkling them with a fine vitamin powder before offering them to your iguanid pets. A simple way to do this is to place a few mealworms in a small container, add a little of the powder, close the lid, and shake gently. The powder will adhere to the mealworms's bodies.

You can obtain mealworms at virtually any pet shop that sells reptiles and amphibians, or perhaps you may want to consider breeding them yourself. To do this, place a number of them in a shallow tray or box containing a layer (5 cm/2 in deep) of bran or other cereal (they love mueseli if you can afford it) and cover the container with a piece of cloth. One or two pieces of carrot or potato placed on the cloth and changed every couple of days will help maintain humidity and provide moisture. The best results are

Most iguanids will take their meals without fuss and can be relied upon to follow a regular feeding schedule. Those specimens that are new to captivity, however, may need some time to adapt. Adult specimens, like this *Sauromalus hispidus*, are often stubborn for the first few weeks. Young specimens, on the other hand, are usually trouble free. Photo by R. D. Bartlett.

obtained when the cultures are maintained at 26 to 30°C/79 to 86°F. A further culture should be started each month, with a few beetles from the first culture, until you have four cultures at various stages of development. The worms in the first culture will pupate and emerge as adult beetles, ready to mate, lay eggs, and repeat the cycle. After about 8 weeks, you will have a new generation of mealworms. Each month, a new culture is started from insects in the oldest culture, which is then discarded. If you keep four cultures at various stages of development, you will have mealworms of varying sizes and maturity, and all of them can be used as food for insectivorous iguanids.

Fruitflies are also a good source of iguanid nutrition and are especially useful in the feeding of small specimens. Fruitflies are those tiny (usually) reddish insects (*Drosophila* spp.) which congregate and breed in rotten fruit. A colony can be started easily enough (in the summer) by placing a box of banana skins or rotten fruit in a remote corner of a garden. In a very short time, the box will be teeming with flies. The flies can be captured using a fine mesh net, and then they should be transferred directly into the terrarium. Because they have such a rapid breeding cycle, fruitflies are used extensively in genetic research. Laboratories culture them in jars of agar jelly and the lab workers can often be persuaded to part with a few cultures and instructions on their further proliferation. Cultures are also sold by biological supply houses and some pet shops.

Perhaps the most often sold livefood, at least in conjunction with lizards, are the crickets. Familiar to everyone, the value of crickets as a cultivatable livefood is quite impressive. Consequently, cultures of these insects have become readily available through the pet trade.

Crickets are a highly nutritious source of food for captive iguanids. Though there are many species of cricket, the two most commonly cultured are the field cricket, *Acheta*, and the domestic cricket, *Gryllus*. They can be kept in suitable containers (plastic sweater box, aquarium tank, etc.) with rolls of corrugated cardboard, balls of newspaper, or old egg boxes in which they can hide. A small saucer containing a piece of wet cotton wadding or a moistened sponge will provide drinking water, and they can be fed on bran or other cereal, plus a little greenfood. A shallow container of damp sand or vermiculite should

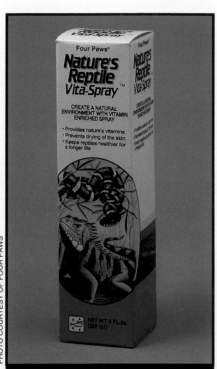

PHOTO COURTESY OF FOUR PAWS

For an added dose of nutrition, a keeper can purchase a vitamin spray that can be used directly on an iguanid's skin. Vitamin sprays promote longer life in captive herptiles plus they prevent drying out of the skin.

BURKHARD KAHL

Crickets probably are the most commonly offered item for captive lizards. Crickets form a complete meal and can be purchased in a variety of sizes. You can also gut-load them or sprinkle them with vitamin powder.

be provided as an egglaying site for the females. At regular intervals, the egglaying accommodation should be removed to a separate container and replaced with a new one. Kept at a temperature of about 25°C/77°F, the eggs will hatch in about 3 weeks. The newly hatched nymphs are about 3 mm/⅛ in long and very suitable as food for hatchling iguanids. There are other nymphal stages, each preceded by a complete skin molt and each a little larger in body size than the former, providing various sizes for your iguanids. The maximum adult length (ordinarily) is about 15 mm/⅝ in.

To remove the crickets from their container, pick up a piece of the material in which they are hiding and shake the insects out into a jar. If placed in the refrigerator for ten minutes or so, they will be subdued enough to prevent escapees when feeding them to your iguanids.

Locusts are usually available from specialist suppliers and can be obtained in various instar sizes ranging from about 5 mm/¼ in to the adult size of 5 cm/2 in. Adult locusts are excellent food for medium-sized insectivorous iguanids, and the nymphs are useful for juveniles. Locusts are not quite as easy to breed as crickets, so you may elect just to purchase them when needed. They are best kept at a temperature of 26 to 30°C/79 to 86°F, in a tall, well-ventilated glass tank. They can be fed on a mixture of bran and crushed oats, supplemented by fresh greenfood. Grass is a convenient greenfood which can be placed into a locust

W. P. MARA

Mealworms are a good supplementary item for captive iguanids (smaller specimens, that is), but should not be offered as a staple item, for they are not nutritionally complete.

tank and kept fresh by placing the stems in a bottle of water with wadding packed around the bottle's neck to prevent the insects from falling in and drowning.

There are other invertebrate foods one can consider as well. The quest for variety in feeding captive terrarium animals has led to many recent experiments concerning the culture of suitable food species. Many species may be purchased and/or bred, so it is up to the individual to decide how much effort he or she is prepared to devote to feeding his or her iguanids. Invertebrates that may be available as cultures include earthworms, whiteworms, snails (various species), wax moths, flour moths, grain beetles, weevils, cockroaches, and stick insects. Purchased cultures are usually offered with instructions on how to proliferate them.

Although thought of most often as a snake food, mice are also accepted by many iguanids; larger omnivorous iguanids will, after all, require more substantial animal food than invertebrates. The consistent availability of laboratory or pet shop mice makes these animals an easily obtainable item for the keeper. It is a matter of personal preference whether you want to purchase your mouse supply or culture them yourself. If you prefer the former, mice can be purchased from laboratories, pet shops, or specialist suppliers; the latter may even supply them in dead, deep-frozen form which can be thawed out and fed to the reptiles when necessary.

Another warm-blooded item you may want to consider is the domestic chick. Hatchling chicks of domestic fowl may be obtained inexpensively from hatcheries either alive or dead (sometimes deep-frozen), and pigeons or quail may also be useful.

## FRUIT AND VEGETABLE FOODS

Many iguanids are strongly herbivorous and will take varying amounts of fruit and vegetable matter. Even some species generally considered to be mainly carnivorous will take soft fruits or grated vegetables every now and then. Most of the common domestic fruits, salads, and vegetables are suitable. By experimenting with a variety, a feeding strategy can be formulated. Lettuce, cabbage (shredded), carrots (grated), tomatoes, capsicums, cucumbers, apples, pears, bananas, grapes, oranges, and boiled potatoes can all be tried. Some specimens may have strange tastes and will require a degree of experimentation before you discover their particular preferences. Fickle feeders can usually be tempted with such items as dandelion (*Taraxacum*) flowers, rose petals, fresh strawberries, canned peaches, lychees, or peas. Species such as the Desert Iguana, *Dipsosaurus dorsalis*, which feed on pungent desert plants in the wild, may often be tempted with plants such as mint or rosemary.

## OTHER FOODS

Although not a regular occurrence, some iguanids will accept pieces of lean meat, heart, or liver (minced for the smaller individuals). Mixing these meats with raw egg (including the crushed shell) often makes them more appealing. Canned dog or cat food may also incite some interest, but these items are usually more of a hindrance than help and should consequently be avoided.

Supplements

No single food item should make up an iguanid's diet completely. If for some reason you find yourself unable to provide more than just one item, then a suitable vitamin/mineral supplement must be included. Such powders can be quite easily added to meat by being scoured into it. Ask your veterinarian or enquire at your pet shop or pharmacy as to which brands of vitamin/mineral powder are most suitable. Supplements should be given to all insectivorous and herbivorous iguanids on a regular basis (say twice per week) by sprinkling the powder onto the food.

## FEEDING STRATEGIES

Smaller iguanids generally need to feed more often than larger ones. Small insectivores and all herbivores should be fed daily, while most of the larger carnivores will get by with three or four meals per week. It is difficult to lay down any hard and fast rules regarding quantities. Aim at keeping the diet balanced without overfeeding; obesity is a common cause of death in captive reptiles. A certain amount of experimentation will be required before you arrive at a suitable routine.

# IN SICKNESS AND IN HEALTH

As responsible keepers, we must never forget the fact that our captives rely on us and us alone for the successful maintenance of their physical (and mental) well-being. In the wild, a sick animal has some chance of recovery, but not much. In captivity, the situation is not quite as bleak, but the margin of improvement is still quite small. Therefore, it is the responsibility of the keeper to deal with disease in only one way—by making sure it never even starts.

## HYGIENE

In essence, hygiene is the science of disease prevention. Always remember that disease organisms will, if given the chance, spread quickly among populations of captive animals. It is therefore our responsibility to practice hygienic measures on a regular basis to ensure that our animals are always in peak health. Each keeper will have his or her own methods of sanitation so there's no point in discussing any others; I do not wish to deviate you from your present mode of operation. But it should be pointed out that in order to maintain a reliable level of cleanliness, the keeper must have a degree of self-discipline because such practices take time and patience. If a person feels he or she does not possess this most vital quality, then it is in the best interests of both the animals and the keeper to decline the keeping of iguanids in the first place.

## THE CLEANING PROCESS

To minimize the risk of a disease outbreak, a cage should not only have all the necessary life-support systems but also be maintained in spotlessly clean condition. In the simplest type of terrarium (used for quarantine, hospitalization, rearing juveniles, etc.), absorbent paper may be used as a substrate and can easily be changed each time it becomes soiled. With other substrates, such as sand or gravel, feces must be removed daily using a scoop or small shovel. Iguanid feces are usually semi-solid and easy to pick up (exceptions to this rule usually occur when an animal is ill). Once per month the whole terrarium should be cleaned thoroughly. All materials should be removed and either discarded or scrubbed clean. The interior of the terrarium and its contents should be scrubbed with warm soapy water and a mild disinfectant such as household bleach or povidone-iodine, then thoroughly swilled out with cold, clean water before being dried and then refurnished.

While you are cleaning, the reptiles can be placed in a spare cage or a plastic box. A plastic trash-can is useful for large species. Water for drinking and/or bathing should be changed everyday. The glass viewing panels should also be kept crystal clear, for both esthetic and hygienic purposes.

## QUARANTINE

A newly acquired iguanid should always be subjected to a period of quarantine before you introduce it to any of your existing stock. If the animal is still healthy after 21 days in an isolation cage, you can reasonably assume it is "safe." The quarantine cage must have all the usual life-support systems of course, but there is no need for any special decorations; keep it as simple as possible.

## HEALTH PROBLEMS

The old sayings "An ounce of prevention is worth a pound of cure," and "Better safe than sorry" seem to apply very well to the captive-maintenance of iguanids. Think about it: if you keep your iguanids clean, in a stress-free environment, and provide them with an adequate diet, they will remain in good health. Let's face it—most disease outbreaks can be blamed on inadequate captive management.

Unfortunately, in spite of our most excelled efforts to keep our pets in show-quality condition, the occasional disease still crawls to the surface, and in such cases a keeper is advised to confer with a veterinarian. Most modern veterinarians have at least some training and experience in reptile medicine, and even if the one you contact cannot help you, chances are very good that he or she will be able to put you in touch with one who can.

The following are some of the health problems commonly suffered by captive iguanids.

## BACTERIAL DISEASES

There are many types of bacterial diseases that can infect iguanids. One of these, infective salmonellosis, is an intestinal disease that can be transmitted from reptiles to man (especially from freshwater turtles, but some iguanids also are suspect), so it is important that you thoroughly wash your hands after each cleaning or handling session. Although most reptiles usually only act as carriers of this disease, the infection itself will occasionally break out. Symptoms

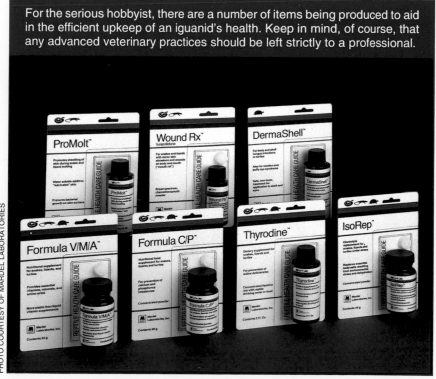

For the serious hobbyist, there are a number of items being produced to aid in the efficient upkeep of an iguanid's health. Keep in mind, of course, that any advanced veterinary practices should be left strictly to a professional.

PHOTO COURTESY OF MARDEL LABORATORIES

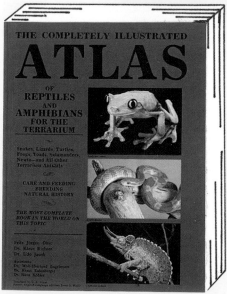

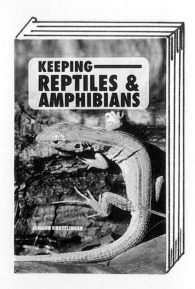

There are a great number of reptile and amphibian books being produced by T.F.H. Publications. T.F.H. is the largest publisher of animal books in the world. Check your local pet shop for titles.

include watery, green-colored, feces; lethargy; and a refusal to feed. Some of the most commonly encountered bacterial diseases in iguanids are caused by gram-negative bacteria such as *Pseudomonas* and *Aeromonas*. Another unpleasant bacterial condition, which usually starts with an injury to the mouth, is mouth rot or infectious ulcerative stomatitis. Most bacterial infections will require antibiotic treatment, so a veterinarian should most definitely be consulted.

### RESPIRATORY INFECTIONS

Unfortunately fairly common with captive iguanids, respiratory infections occur very often in highly stressed specimens or specimens that are exposed to cold drafts. The patient will have difficulty breathing, the nostrils will be blocked, and there will be a nasal discharge. The discharge should be washed away with a mild antiseptic solution and the patient should be moved to a warmer, drier, terrarium. More serious cases will require antibiotic treatment from a veterinarian.

### TICKS AND MITES

These are the two most commonly encountered ectoparasites as far as captive reptiles are concerned.

Ticks often are found attached to newly captured iguanids and may range up to 5 mm/¼ in in length. In order to feed on the blood of their victims, ticks will use their piercing mouthparts to fasten onto secluded spots between the scales—often around the vent, below the neck, or where the limbs join the body. Do not recklessly attempt to pull a tick out of an iguanid's body because there is the chance that the tick's head may remain embedded in the skin, causing further infection later on. Instead, dab the tick's body with a

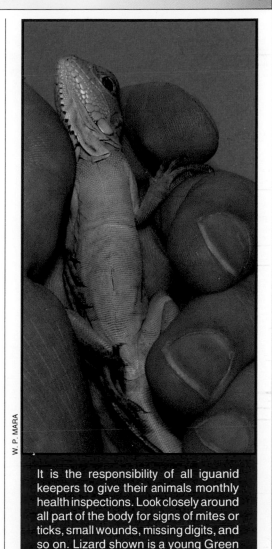

W. P. MARA

It is the responsibility of all iguanid keepers to give their animals monthly health inspections. Look closely around all part of the body for signs of mites or ticks, small wounds, missing digits, and so on. Lizard shown is a young Green Iguana, *Iguana iguana*.

little alcohol (isopropyl, methanol, or even a drop of whiskey). This will cause the attached mouthparts to relax. After this is accomplished the tick then can be pulled out gently but firmly with the thumb and forefinger, or with forceps. Once all ticks have been removed, a further infestation in the terrarium is unlikely.

Mites are more serious than ticks since they can multiply into large numbers before you even notice them. Mites do not stay on a reptile's body at all times; they usually hide in crevices in the terrarium during the day and come out during the night. If mites are allowed to grow into a small army, an iguanid host will suffer from stress, anemia, sloughing problems, loss of appetite, and very possibly death. Mites are also capable of transmitting blood-pathogenic organisms from one reptile to another. A single mite is smaller than a pinhead, roughly globular in shape, and grayish in color, becoming red after it has taken a blood meal. In a heavily infested terrarium, mites may be seen running about even during the "lights-on" hours. Also, silvery, powdery droppings may be seen on the reptile's skin. Mites are almost always introduced into a terrarium by way of new stock that was infested to begin with (another good reason for quarantine and careful inspection).

Fortunately, mites can be quickly eradicated through the use of a insecticidal strip of the type used to control houseflies. A small piece of such a strip placed in a perforated container and suspended in the terrarium will do the trick. Remove the strip after two days, then repeat the process ten days later to kill off any newly hatched mites. This treatment usually destroys all mites in the terrarium. Remember that you shouldn't leave a strip in a cage for too long or it may do harm to the iguanids themselves.

### WORM INFESTATIONS

Endoparasitic worms are organisms that live inside the body, usually in the alimentary tract, where they thrive on the partially digested food of the host. Although there are many parasitic worms, roundworms and tapeworms are the ones most likely to found in iguanids. Nearly all wild reptiles are infested with worms

DR. FREDRIC L. FRYE IN *REPTILE CARE*

Ectoparasites are commonly found on captive iguanids, particularly ticks and mites. Most cases can be taken care of easily enough as long as the problem is noticed in its early stages.

of one form or another, and in most cases there is no danger to the reptiles; after all, it is not in the worms's interest to kill their host! However, during times of stress (capture for example), normal resistance to such infestation will be lessened, triggering a massive increase in size and/or numbers of worms, thus causing anemia, general lethargy, loss of appetite, and eventually death.

Worms are continually laying eggs that are passed out of the host's body via the feces. These eggs will then hatch and the new worms will be ready to invade yet another animal. By executing a routine microscopic examination of your iguanid's fecal samples in a veterinary laboratory (say, every few months), you will be able to spot any infestations before they get out of hand. There are several vermicides available through your veterinarian that may be offered with food or, in severe cases, via stomach tube.

## PROTOZOAN INFECTIONS

Parasitic protozoan organisms such as *Entamoeba invadens* can cause various enteric infections. If untreated, a disease caused by such organisms can rapidly reach epidemic proportions in captive reptiles. Symptoms include watery, slimy feces and general debilitation. Treatment with metronidazole (by a veterinarian) via stomach tube has proven effective.

## NUTRITIONAL DEFICIENCIES

A lack of only one or two essential vitamins or minerals in an iguanid's diet can very easily place the animal's health in jeopardy, especially in the case of growing juveniles, who could easily develop rickets and bone malformations. However, with a correct variety of foods, vitamin and mineral supplements, fresh water, and an opportunity to bask in real or artificial sunlight, such conditions will be prevented.

## WOUNDS AND INJURIES

Though not really "diseases" in the standard sense, wounds caused by fights with cagemates, escape attempts, and so forth are susceptible to infection and must be treated immediately. Shallow wounds usually will heal fairly quickly and without further problem if swabbed daily with a mild antiseptic such as povidone-iodine. More serious wounds should only be treated by a veterinarian because in many cases surgery, suturing, and antibiotic treatment may be required.

## SKIN PROBLEMS

One of the most common causes of skin infections in iguanids is the animal's inability to slough properly. This is often the result of a mite infestation or of stress brought about by various other factors (including low humidity or a lack of bathing facilities).

Most healthy reptiles will shed their skins without any problems several times per year; it is a natural phenomenon related to growth. In iguanids (and other lizards as well), the skin is normally shed in patches. The whole process usually does not take more than a few days. Disease organisms can multiply behind patches of old skin that will not come off, but such patches usually can be loosened off by placing the animal in a bath of very shallow warm water for about an hour or so. If the patches do not loosen and become unstuck on their own, they can be very gently peeled off with the fingers. If the patch still remains adherent, try dabbing it with a drop of mineral oil, rubbing the oil in well, then attempting to peel again.

Another skin problem is abscesses, which appear as lumps below the skin. Abscesses are usually caused by subcutaneous infections that build up after the skin has been accidentally damaged. Abscesses should be treated only by a veterinarian since they are very delicate and demand a trained, experienced hand. A severe abscess may have to be surgically incised, cleaned up, and then sutured, ultimately followed by the administration of medication.

# MISCELLANEOUS TOPICS

There are a few minor topics that can be applied to the keeping of iguanids, most of which really can't be included in any of the other chapters presented thus far. Therefore, I have decided to include these topics in a chapter of their own. Each one involves ideals which you as an iguanid enthusiast will definitely be able to relate to and further apply to your future endeavors. Hopefully, they will help you become a better hobbyist as well, or at the very least, a more knowledgeable one.

## ACQUIRING YOUR IGUANIDS

As an enthusiast of iguanids, one of your first and foremost concerns should be that you acquire healthy livestock from the start. To ensure this, always give a potential specimen a thorough examination before purchasing it: look for signs of mites or ticks on the skin; choose only those specimens with a sleek, unbroken skin and no lumps, cysts, or sores; and ensure that the reptile is clear-eyed, alert, and plump. Look for broken claws or damage to the tail. Examine the nose, mouth, and vent for any signs of discharges that could indicate disease or abnormality. Ask if the reptile is feeding regularly and on what because you will need to continue with a similar diet or gradually wean it onto a new one.

There are three main sources from which you can obtain iguanids: pet shops, breeders, or importers. Whatever means you choose, be sure you are not breaking any conservation laws; many reptile species are highly protected. It is only by having a responsible attitude to our wildlife that we can hope to preserve it. Laws may vary from country to country, or even from state to state or town to town, so make sure you are aware of the legislation pertaining to your area. You can usually get this information free of charge from government bodies.

Of all the aforementioned sources for obtaining iguanid specimens, the best one is undoubtedly the breeder; you will then be sure the animal is you get captive-bred and thus will have a great adaptability to captivity. It is also more likely to be healthy and willing to eat. You may even get to know the history of the animal's pedigree, however brief it may be. The final positive aspect of acquiring a captive-bred specimen means that it is one more that wasn't taken from the wild.

## TRANSPORTING YOUR IGUANIDS

Iguanids are normally transported in cloth bags, which in turn are placed in stout cardboard boxes in the case of smaller specimens, or wooden boxes for larger ones. Each reptile is best placed individually in a separate cloth bag, and then a number of these bags may be placed in a transport box. With larger iguanids, ensure that each individual has its own compartment. Try not to transport iguanids in very cold weather, but if you must, arrange for some kind of temporary heating and/ or insulation (styrofoam containers or liners are ideal). After the iguanids reach their destination they should be housed appropriately as soon as possible. If you are transporting an iguanid home from its place of purchase, it is acceptable to simply carry it in a bag, provided of course the air temperature is not too low and the journey is a short one. Also, you should not leave an iguanid in a car in the hot sun. Iguanids can indeed become overheated in such a situation and quickly expire.

### HANDLING IGUANIDS

Handling techniques differ depending on the size of an iguanid, but most specimens will become relatively easy to deal with once they get to know you. Small iguanids simply may be grasped in the palm of the hand.

They may try to bite, but these bites are usually quite harmless. Be gentle and remember that many iguanids's tails will snap off if the animals are handled too roughly around that area of their anatomy. Large specimens should be treated with greater caution and respect because they not only have a powerful bite, but sharp claws and powerful whiplike tails as well; in short, they can hurt you. Such iguanids are best restrained by gripping their necks with one hand and extending their fingers to secure their front limbs, while their rear limbs and tail are restrained by tucking them under your elbow. Some specimens, especially those reared and handled frequently from juvenile age, are

The key to correctly handling an iguanid is *give it as much bodily support as possible.* (Although, with really large animals, this, of course, may be next to impossible.) Photo by Isabelle Francais.

usually very tame and thus no problem at all to handle, even when fully grown.

### HIBERNATING IGUANIDS

Iguanids from temperate and sub-tropical climates invariably hibernate for varying periods of time. In the wild, they seek out hibernation spots far enough below ground to escape the ravages of the frost, and many species can withstand remarkably low temperatures.

Hibernation is a natural part of a reptile's life cycle and helps bring many species into breeding condition. In the past, many captive iguanids were kept in "active" temperatures throughout the year, but herpetologists generally

agree today that non-tropical reptiles should be given at least some artificial hibernation if they are going to be bred. Hibernating your pets may not seem like a very exciting prospect since they will not be seen

Green Iguanas, *Iguana iguana*, especially larger specimens, don't seem to care much for handling, and some can give you very nasty scratches, so beware. Photo by Isabelle Francais.

for quite a while, but with some species a short "rest-period" at lower temperatures seems to be an adequate substitute for full hibernation. Only healthy, well-fed specimens should be hibernated. As winter approaches, stop feeding your stock and reduce the temperature gradually over a period of several days. The photoperiod also should be gradually reduced during this time. The minimum temperature will vary from 10°C/50°F for temperate-climate species to 20°C/60°F for sub-tropical species. Once the exact temperature has been realized it should not be altered. Hibernation for iguanids can last anywhere from 4 to 8 weeks, perhaps a little longer for the most northerly ranging species. Once the hibernation period is over, the temperature should then be raised gradually, as should the photoperiod, until the animals are returned to their "normal active" state.

If you are really serious about owning a Green Iguana, *Iguana iguana*, that you want to handle often, it is strongly advised that you buy your specimen when it is very young. Older specimens tend to be more "set in their ways" and may never get used to being handled. Photo by Isabelle Francais.

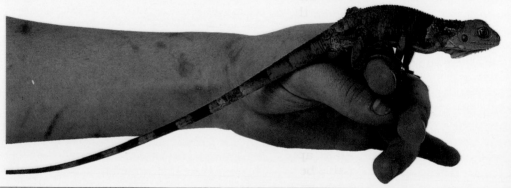

# THE GREEN IGUANA, *IGUANA IGUANA*

Undoubtedly, the most famous of all iguanids deserves a chapter all to itself. Indeed this magnificent creature is the one most people recognize as "The Iguana." It is one of the most popular of all pet lizards (in fact, of on the most popular herptiles overall) and has been imported into many countries for just this purpose. By devoting a chapter to this species alone I will be able to cover the many aspects of its natural history and care in greater detail.

## DESCRIPTION

Reaching an average adult length of up to 180 cm/6 ft (although some specimens have been know to reach 210 cm/7 ft) the Green Iguana is a slender-bodied lizard with a long, laterally flattened tail. In cross-section, the body is an upright oval. The head is relatively large and the snout is rounded. The limbs are well-developed and the digits are armed with sharp nails. They have a conspicuous, serrated, erectable dewlap under the chin and throat, and a characteristic of the species is a group of enlarged scales just below the ear (tympanum), one in particular being very large and obvious. (In the rarely seen Antillean Iguana, *Iguana delicatissima*, the only other species of the genus, these scales are greatly reduced and the aforementioned "central" scale is nonexistent.) There is a crest of spikey dorsal spines extending from the neck to the first third of the tail.

The color is predominantly green to grayish, darkening with age so that very old specimens may appear almost black. (It should also be noted that selective captive breeding has also produced a fairly blue *Iguana iguana* as well.) There are darker bands across the shoulders and tail and there may be a bluish tinge around the upper forelimbs. The scales below the prominent external eardrum are usually whitish with a tinge of green. The ventrum is lighter green to off-white. Some specimens also show splashes of reddish brown to yellow on various parts of the body.

Male and female Green Iguanas are fairly similar in appearance, but there are some noticeable differences. For example, the male's dewlap and crests are generally larger and a male's head is more robust and the coloration and patterns are more vivid. Also, there is a row of well-developed glandular pores under the hind thighs (these are only vestigial in the females). Juveniles of both gender are almost wholly bright grass-green in color with the crest and dewlap being poorly developed.

## RANGE

The Green Iguana thrives in suitable habitats from northern Mexico through Central America and into South America around the Tropic of Capricorn, plus a number of small islands off the pacific Gulf and Atlantic Coasts. There are also introduced and thriving populations in Florida and on the northeastern coast of Puerto Rico. Due to overcollection and loss of habitat, the Green Iguana has become very scarce and in some cases extirpated from many of its former haunts.

## HABITS AND HABITATS

The Green Iguana is most at home in the trees and never far from water. It is an extremely adept climber, using its strong claws to scale the trunks and limbs of trees with ease. It prefers trees with a large, green canopy and will rest or bask on limbs overhanging water, into which it will dive if threatened. If there is no direct access to water, a Green Iguana will drop from a tree to the ground and land on all fours, then scuttle off for cover with remarkable speed.

The Green Iguana is almost as much at home in the water as in the trees. When escaping from predators, it dives deeply, using its long, flattened, undulating tail to propel itself in the direction of cover. It is believed the limbs are not used for swimming propulsion but instead for stabilization and turning. A Green Iguana will hide among aquatic vegetation or between the submerged roots of waterside trees and shrubs, only bringing its head and nostrils above the surface when it is assured the danger has passed.

The tail is used extensively as an instrument of balance during the animal's climbing activities. Although the tail is not exactly prehensile (fitted for grasping or holding), it is used as a steadying or thrusting aid in various circumstances. Another function of the tail involves defense—it is aimed at a potential adversary and used in a whiplike fashion. Anyone who has had a lash across the face from a Green Iguana's tail will vouch for its efficiency in this function! If cornered or gripped, the Green Iguana not only uses its tail in defense, but its sharp claws are also capable of ripping into the human skin. Its rows of serrated teeth are to be treated with great respect as well. Thankfully, such feisty defensive behavior usually is soon lost by captive specimens (although a keeper should always be aware that unpredictable behavior can still occur).

Like many lizards, Green Iguanas can shed most or part of their tail—a process known as *autotomy*—but they do not perform this function as readily as some other lizard species (some of which can do it voluntarily). The tail breaks at a point of pre-existing weakness on the tail vertebrae (not between two vertebrae as was once thought). In many lizard species, autotomy is an aid to defense—the lizard makes its escape while the predator is dealing with the wriggling, snapped-off tail. In the case of the Green Iguana, and probably many other members of the Iguanidae as well, the tail is cast off only as a last resort. I experienced this once when an escaped specimen jammed itself behind a hot radiator. I had to remove the animal before it was severely burned, but the only part it I could get a proper grip on was the tail. I decided to take the risk and began pulling with gradually increasing pressure. Suddenly the tail broke and I was left holding it as it wriggled about in my hands. The rest of the animal was eventually levered out using a broomstick. It was a sorry sight—a nice Green Iguana with only a bloody stump for a tail, plus a few minor burns on one of its flanks and thighs. For a few weeks the reptile was very unhappy and refused food, but in time it grew a passable replacement tail which was much shorter than the original and uniform gray in color. The burns also healed well, but left their signature as permanent, shiny scar tissue. Thus, in view of my experience, I would strongly recommend that no Green Iguana is ever lifted by the tail!

Adult wild Green Iguanas feed on a variety of plant foods, including young shoots, leaves, flowers, and fruits.

They will also occasionally take invertebrates, small vertebrates (nestling birds for example), and carrion. In other words, Green Iguanas can be regarded as primarily herbivorous creatures that turn carnivorous. A good example of this is illustrated by what I experienced when I once worked as a reptile curator in a zoological park. It was necessary every now and then to enter the reptile house at night to check on various things, and the house was infested with large cockroaches that enjoyed the warmth, humidity, and abundant food supply. These cockroaches were rarely seen during the day because they hid themselves in various service ducts, but when I turned on the lights at night they were quite obvious. If I turned on the lights in the Green Iguana cage, the inmates were instantly awoken and would scuttle after any cockroaches that had come into their confinement. With great delight, they would go after each victim before even finishing up the previous one. The young were particularly insectivorous during their early growth periods, feeding on a variety of invertebrates and only a small amount of plant food. The tendency to be herbivorous increases as a Green Iguana matures and the animal's diet eventually finishes off with a rough plant/animal food ratio of approximately 6:1.

Green Iguanas live in tropical and sub-tropical areas only and do not necessarily hibernate as such, but if the daytime temperature drops below 20°C/68°F they will retire to a burrow or tree hollow and remain fairly torpid until the temperature improves. They like to bask in radiant sunlight on colder days, presumably in an attempt to procure as much warmth as possible. They seem to be quite comfortable in environmental temperatures of up to 33°C/92°F during the day, but would, of course, be unable to tolerate this all day and all night. The critical maximum body temperature of the Green Iguana is somewhere around 35°C/95°F; anywhere above that and the reptile very likely would not survive. They are most active when they have reached their preferred daytime body temperature of around 33°C/91°F. Like all lizards, Green Iguanas maintain their temperature by moving their bodies in and out of warm areas.

## SOME CONSIDERATIONS OF CONSERVATION IN THE WILD

Green Iguanas are preyed upon by a variety of animals. Snakes, including anacondas and Boa Constrictors, will take larger specimens while juvenile Green Iguanas are preyed upon by these and other snake species. Caimans, large freshwater turtles, and even large freshwater fish, all play a part in the periodic consumption of Green Iguanas, as do certain birds and carnivorous mammals, including otters, bears, jaguars, and other wildcats. Also, Amerindian tribes have included Green Iguanas on their menus for generations. However, it should be pointed out that, relatively speaking, all of these predators combined have very little impact on Green Iguana populations since they are a part of the animal's natural ecology.

The arrival of European man on the South American continent, however, spelled disaster for many animal species. Human populations have increased, and thus thousands of acres of habitat have been destroyed. Natural sites for Green Iguanas have been replaced by housing developments, mines, factories, wharves, agricultural areas, ball parks, and so on. The Amerindians still continue to eat the Green Iguanas that are left, as do many of the pets belonging to the "new" Americans, i.e., cats, dogs, and so on. And if that isn't enough, collectors still continue to capture them and sell them as pets.

As well as using dogs, nets, darts, arrows, clubs, and guns to catch or kill Green Iguanas, hunters also exploit the subtleties of the Iguana's own habitat in order to capture them. For example: on hearing the sound of a bird of prey, a Green Iguana will usually "freeze," hoping its camouflage will protect it. Thus, by imitating the sound of, say, a hawk, a hunter can make a close approach and easily catch the reptile. Another method is for a number of collectors to follow a river bank inhabited by Green Iguanas, then, while one climbs a tree to frighten the reptiles into the water, the others will be swimming in the river below ready to collect them. The specimens are rather barbarically carried off by threading a cord or pole through the tendons of their hind limbs, and are then offered for sale this way in the markets.

Fortunately, many countries have now seen the importance of preserving their wildlife, and Green Iguanas are at last being protected— they are listed in the appendices of the Convention on International Trade in Endangered Species of Wild Flora and Fauna (CITES). This means that the international trade of this species is only allowed under special license, and even then there are strict regulations with regard to the capture, restraint, husbandry, and transport of specimens. All of this is, of course, a big reason why captive breeding of our reptiles is of utmost importance. If the species becomes even more scarce (as it inevitably will), then the breeding of captive stock will be the only way to produce further specimens for the enthusiasts.

## CAPTIVE HUSBANDRY

Even the smallest Green Iguana specimens still require a fairly large terrarium. In the case of large adult specimens, it is preferable to give them their own heated room or greenhouse, complete with a deep pool. If it has to be a terrarium, I would recommend a minimum size of 180 cm wide x 180 cm high x 90 cm deep, or, approximately 6 ft x 6 ft x 3 ft, for a pair of adults; larger if possible. In a smaller terrarium, a large water bath is essential; a plastic baby's bathtub or similar can be useful. Since Green Iguanas drink and bathe often, it is essential that the water is replaced as frequently as possible. When it is necessary to keep them in smaller cages, it is recommended that they be allowed out to exercise regularly. You will find that they like to clamber over things, so it goes without saying that you should remove any valuables and hide all the house plants. During the summer you can allow your Green Iguanas to get plenty of fresh air and sunshine by taking them outside. You can either place them in a chicken coop-type structure on the lawn, or, if they are tame enough, you can allow them to forage in a small tree or shrub. Do not let them out of your sight, however, otherwise they are likely to give some neighbor a heart attack!

Robust climbing branches should be provided in the terrarium since Green Iguanas enjoy them and will spend much time climbing on them. Don't forget to fasten the branches securely to the walls to prevent accidents. It will be a waste of time to put living plants in the enclosure because the inmates will eat or damage them. Pea-sized gravel is an acceptable substrate material, or, if you have an impermeable floor, (concrete, treated timber, vinyl, etc.), you may want to simply leave it bare since it will be easy to keep clean by hosing and scrubbing. The air temperature should be kept in the range of 25 to 30°C/77 to 86°F during the day with a further facility to bask under an infra-red heat lamp. At night the temperature can be reduced to as low as 22°C/72°F but not too much lower or else the animals may develop hypothermia. A medium amount of humidity is required and will usually be automatic if there is an adequate water bath. Good ventilation is essential and can be facilitated by placing an aquarium airstone, connected to an air pump, into the enclosure's water body. This will keep the air circulating and also promote humidity.

Full-spectrum lighting most definitely should be provided, especially during the winter when the lizards will not be getting much (if any) natural sunlight. Ultra-violet light on its own is not recommended unless you provide about 20 minutes of it two or three times a week; over-exposure to ultra-violet rays is very dangerous! Needless to say, you should always be sure that all electrical fittings are inaccessible from the animals and not in any way in contact with a water body. If in doubt, hire an electrician to do the job!

## FEEDING

The adult Green Iguana is about 80% herbivorous, which probably makes life easier on the keeper (who, on the other hand, might instead own animal that thrives on livefoods such as mice, crickets, and so on). You will find that they will accept such items as fresh clover, lucerne, dandelion (leaves and flowers), lettuce, and spinach as a staple diet, supplemented with various fruits and berries such as tomatoes, cucumbers, apples, pears, pineapples, peaches, apricots, strawberries, gooseberries, blackcurrents, cherries, plums, avocados, and so forth. You can also try such items as grated carrots, sweet potatoes, pumpkins, boiled potatoes, zucchinis, peas, beans, cabbages, broccoli, and perhaps a few others. You will find that not all Green Iguanas will eat every item I've listed so you may have to deal with a certain amount of experimentation before you arrive at an ideal diet for your particular animal(s). And remember, canned fruit (pears, peaches, fruit salad, etc.) can often convert a "bad feeder" into a "good feeder."

Since I said the Green Iguana was 80% herbivorous, I suppose it would be natural for reader to wonder about that other 20%. In short, it is mostly invertebrate foods such as mealworms, grasshoppers, crickets, and cockroaches. Additionally, a Green Iguana may be given the occasional meal of minced lean beef, ox heart, and canned cat or dog food. I once had a specimen that was crazy about half-grown mice.

Also, a multi-vitamin/mineral supplement powder regularly should be sprinkled over all the foods. I would recommend a daily dish of mixed vegetable food, with the addition of meat and insects twice per week and the vitamin/mineral supplement also twice per week. And remember not to overfeed your pets either. A lot of keepers seem to think a Green Iguana that loves to eat should be fed by the shovelful. This is not so. In reality, there is nothing wrong with leaving your specimens just a little hungry. That way, they'll be more eager to take the next feeding.

### BREEDING

The practice of successfully breeding Green Iguanas in captivity has seen a marked increase in popularity over the last few years, but it is still not done frequently enough to meet the demands of the pet industry. The success of the process seems to revolve around the stimulus garnered by introducing a new male to an existing pair. By keeping two males and two females, and keeping them apart except when breeding them, it is likely that you will end up with both females gravid. Conversely, a male/female pair kept together for too long will often go for years with no attempt at breeding—perhaps never at all!

A brief word should be said about Green Iguanas in regards to hibernation for those of you who are curious and do not have all the facts. Green Iguanas, *Iguana iguana*, do not hibernate in the standard sense of the word. Studies have shown that specimens given an ambient temperature of under 16°C/60°F without any place in which to warm themselves die in a few weeks's time. Therefore, if you are keeping Green Iguanas, it is suggested that you simply lower there overall temperature only slightly and let that, coupled with a reduction in photoperiod, act as one of the catalysts for the reproductive cycle.

In the wild, male Green Iguanas are extremely territorial, taking up an area of river bank with several trees and defending it vigorously against any other males. During such a confrontation, the defending male raises up his body by stretching out his limbs and directs the curved side of his body towards the intruder. At the same time, his dewlap is extended and visibly darkens in color. Should the threat fail to impress the intruder (which would cause him to take a passive stance by crouching low or simply move away), the intruder himself will take on a similar stance. Then, first circling each other warily, they will eventually come to blows by banging their heads together. During these fascinating fights, the males rarely, if ever, injure each other. Most of the procedure is simply bluff. Eventually, one of the opponents will give up and the victor is left to mate with the female.

By introducing two pairs together in the terrarium, you can experience a similar ritual, then you can return the visiting pair back to their original accommodations before either male has had a chance to begin the combat. This very often will fool both males into thinking they have won the battle and thus will proceed to court and mate with their respective females.

Green Iguana courtship consists of head-nodding and dewlap-spreading by both sexes. The male eventually takes the female by the neck in his mouth, and if she is receptive to his desires she will allow him to pass his cloacal region under hers, holding her tail with one of his hind legs as he does so. He then inserts one of his hemipenes into her cloaca, and copulation takes place for 5 to 45 minutes.

It is interesting to note that female Green Iguanas may also perform a threat ritual similar to the males's outlined above, but this is usually only in order to protect their sleeping branches or fight for the best egglaying sites.

After a fertile mating, a female Green Iguana will be gravid for 50 to 100 days depending on temperature, humidity, food supply, and so on. To a certain extent, therefore, egg development can be hastened or slowed by the keeper if need be. 2 or 3 weeks before the eggs are deposited, the female ceases to feed but will take in increasing amounts of water.

In the wild, suitable nesting areas often are scarce. The female will take into account the aspect of the sun, the ease with which the subsoil can be excavated, and the general safety of the area. To avoid egg-predation by humans and domestic and wild animals, gravid Green Iguanas often swim relatively long distances to uninhabited islands in rivers and estuaries. They lay their eggs in burrows along sunny banks above the high water mark. They excavate these burrows with their front limbs, pushing the damp, sandy soil back with their rear limbs until the hole is 1 to 2 m/3 to 6 ft long and the egglaying chamber is about 60 cm/2 ft below ground level. After laying the eggs, the female fills in the burrow and then returns to her usual habitat. The average number of eggs in a Green Iguana's clutch is about 20 to 40, but up to 70 have been recorded. The white, leathery eggs are usually laid two at a time, with intervals between the pairs. The dimensions of the slightly oval eggs average about 35 x 25 mm (approximately 1.4 x 1.0 in) and weigh 10 to 12 grams.

In captivity, female Green Iguanas often are not satisfied with the egglaying facilities and will end up just dropping their eggs on the cage floor. If you keep your pets in large enough enclosures you can provide them with a deep sandpit for egglaying. Wherever the eggs are laid, they must be collected for artificial incubation since facilities in the terrarium itself will not be adequate.

## INCUBATION

As I stated above, eggs laid in captivity must be collected and placed in an incubator since conditions in the terrarium are generally unsuitable for development of the embryos. Newly laid eggs often have dimples or collapsed areas, but these will soon fill out as moisture absorption occurs. The eggs should be carefully removed from the terrarium and kept in the same position in which they were found. They are then placed in an incubation box that has been filled with about a two-inch layer of vermiculite. The soft, white, leathery shell absorbs moisture from the substrate or incubation medium. Remember not to bury the eggs more than halfway and, for the sake of convenience, lay them out in neat rows. If you can avoid keeping the eggs in clusters, do so, for any egg that spoils may infect those that are near to it.

As I mentioned before, vermiculite is probably the best substrate medium available to the breeder. This inert, sterile, absorbent, insulating material is available in various grades. For general incubation purposes, a fine grade is used. Moisten the vermiculite until it is damp, but not soggy. The lid of the incubation box should have a few ventilation holes to allow for air circulation, but at the same time, make sure these holes are not too large or else you will not be able to conserve much moisture. Maintain incubation temperature at 28 to 31°C/82 to 88°F.

The type of incubator you use appears to be unimportant as long as the correct temperature range can be provided. Professional incubators can be purchased but are rather expensive. A perfectly satisfactory one can be made with a simple wooden box or an old fish tank as long as either of these contains an incandescent light bulb and a thermostat for temperature regulation. Placing a thermometer in the box will allow you to monitor the temperature. Also, for the supplication of heat, it is best to use a blue or red bulb and mount the bulb in some sort of cover to minimize the light's harshness. Alternatively, a heating pad, cable, or porcelain heater may be used, or, by placing a dish of water in the "incubator" and warming it with an aquarium heater you will be able to increase both heat and humidity.

During development, the eggs will absorb moisture from the surrounding medium and increase in weight. Infertile eggs will not absorb water, but do not discard them until you are quite sure they have spoiled. Duration of incubation will vary from about 90 to 120 days, depending on the temperature and humidity. This incubation period can be quite a boring time for a keeper, but you must squelch the desire to fiddle with your Green Iguana eggs or else you may damage them, and believe me, they are very delicate. Remain stoical, and in time you will have your reward.

When the eggs are finally ready to hatch, the babies will slit through the tough, parchment-like shell with a sharp projection on the snout known as the egg tooth, which is shed shortly after hatching. Sometimes hatching Green Iguanas will take up to 24 hours or more to abandon their eggshell prisons, but the temptation to "help" them should be suppressed unless the reptile is having difficulties that are obviously endangering their health. Occasionally a hatchling will become stuck to its eggshell because the fluids inside the egg dried up before the animal could wriggle free.

You can remedy this problem by gently dabbing the affected parts with cotton wadding soaked in lukewarm water.

### REARING

As soon as Green Iguana hatchlings are detached from their eggshell and are ready to take on the world, they should be removed from the incubation chamber and placed in "nursery" accommodation. This accommodation should be simply furnished and yet still have all the necessary life-support systems one would supply to any other iguanid. Small plastic aquarium tanks with ventilated lids are ideal since they can be placed in a larger heated terrarium or heated separately on heat tapes or pads. High humidity can be maintained by placing a container of water (keep it shallow) in each tank and by mist-spraying twice daily. The babies must have regular access to unfiltered direct sunlight or to full-spectrum lighting (a topic discussed elsewhere in this book) If you notice a yolk sac still attached to your hatchling Green Iguanas, do not attempt to remove it. Once the contents have been absorbed, this sac will shrivel up and drop off on its own, leaving a tiny scar on the animal's belly.

As long as both the correct climatic conditions and the correct food items are provided, hatchling Green Iguanas should start eating within 7 days (prior to this they will still be living on the contents of the yolk sac). A good diet for hatchling Green Iguanas is a mixture of green foods such as lettuce, spinach, dandelion leaves and flowers, alfalfa, and clover, chopped into small pieces. In addition to this you can add some grated carrot, bone-meal, lean mince, and a small amount of vitamin/mineral supplement given at least twice times per week. Additionally, a daily helping of mealworms, crickets, or other collected insects should be given. If certain kinds of food are ignored by your pets, try others until you are successful. Once a youngster starts taking one kind of food, it will not be long before the animal is prepared to try others. It is a good idea to weigh your specimens regularly and monitor their growth progress. Remember to keep records, both for your own use and for the use of others in the future. As Green Iguanas grow they will become increasingly herbivorous until finally they are on a full adult diet. Under optimum conditions, Green Iguanas can reach sexual maturity in 3 years.

## SOME OTHER IGUANIDS

At present, the family Iguanidae contains around two dozen species in eight genera. In a small book such as this, only a few of these species can be discussed in any detail, but the information that is included should give you a better understanding of the family Iguanidae and maybe even urge you to further your hobbyist ambitions.

One of the most interesting species, and one that can claim notoriety as the world's only saltwater lizard, is the Marine Iguana, *Amblyrhynchus cristatus*, of the Galapagos Islands (Ecuador). This lizard lives on the rocky cliffs and headlands of some of the islands, entering the sea frequently to browse on its staple diet of seaweed. It is a large species, growing to 175 cm/69 in, and is an accomplished swimmer. Normally gray-brown in color, the males take on bright red patches during the mating season. Another Galapagos species is the yellowish brown Land Iguana, *Conolophus subcristatus*, a stocky animal

reaching an overall length of around 110 cm/43 in. Unlike the Marine Iguana, it confines itself to the land and feeds on vegetation including cactus. Galapagos iguanas are never likely to be available in the pet market.

Central America is the home of a few species of spiny-tailed iguanas, genus *Ctenosaura*. One of these, *C. pectinata*, has been introduced into parts of Texas and Florida. It is grayish to yellowish brown with broad, darker crossbands. Reaching a total length of 120 cm/48 in, it has a raised crest of scales along its back and a spiny tail that is used in defense. Food and care are similar to those described for the Green Iguana, but with less humid conditions.

The Desert Iguana, *Dipsosaurus dorsalis*, of southwestern USA and adjacent Mexico, is a favorite terrarium pet. Growing to a maximum length of 40 cm/16 in, it has a relatively small head and a plump body. A short-spined crest runs along the back and tail. It is usually light brown to cream in color, marked with darker spots. When basking in the sun, the whole body color lightens. It is primarily herbivorous, but occasionally will take insects. The most preferred foods include pungent herbs such as sage and rosemary, as well as yellow flowers, in preference to the more usual greens. It requires daytime air temperatures in the terrarium of 28 to 32°C/82 to 90°F, with basking temperatures up to 35°C/95°F.

Some of the West Indian islands have their own unique iguanid species. The most spectacular must be the Rhinoceros Iguana, *Cyclura cornuta*, from Haiti and Puerto Rico. This large-headed species has three horns on top of its snout, hence the common name. Growing to about 110 cm/43 in, it is rather plain gray-brown in color. Being a fairly belligerent lizard, it will bite fiercely if given the chance. It is more or less herbivorous with a diet close to that of the Green Iguana, although occasionally *C. cornuta* will take whole dead mice or day old chicks, for example. Another, more colorful, species from Haiti is the slightly larger, Ricord's Iguana, *Cyclura ricordi*, which is a beautiful reddish brown color with a fairly tall crest of spines. Diet and habits similar to Rhinoceros Iguana.

A couple of species that are never likely to be very common in captivity (which is a shame as they are probably the most attractive of all iguanids) are the Pacific Island iguanas (*Brachylophus* spp.) that are found on the islands of Fiji and Tonga and have recently been introduced to Vanuatu. They are believed to be descendants of iguanids from Central or South America that moved across the Pacific and colonized the islands, eventually developing into separate species. The two species are the Banded Iguana, *B. fasciatus*, and the Crested Iguana, *B. vitiensis*. Both reach about 90 cm/36 in in length. The Banded Iguana has a much shorter crest than the Crested. The males are capable of darkening their colors to almost black during courtship or territorial display. Both of these species have similar habits to the Green Iguana, feeding on a wide range of vegetation and some animal food. Both are highly endangered and require strict protection.

Finally, no book about iguanids would be complete without some mention of the Chuckwalla, *Sauromalus obesus*, which ranges through the southwestern USA and into Mexico. Inhabiting open flats and rocky outcrops, it can withstand very high temperatures—it likes to operate with a body temperature of about 38°C/100°F. Growing to 40 cm/16 in, it is a very fat-looking lizard with loose folds of skin around its neck and shoulders. The male has a black head and forequarters, running into red, yellow, or gray toward the rear end and into the shortish tail. The female tends to be banded in gray and off-yellow. It is a strictly herbivorous iguanid, feeding on leaves, flowers, buds, and fruits. When under threat, the Chuckwalla jams itself into a rock crevice by inflating its body, and in such circumstances it is extremely difficult to dislodge. In captivity it requires a desert-type terrarium with basking temperatures to 45°C/104°F, but beware of using "hot rocks" with Chuckwallas because they seem to have a propensity for remaining on them too long and burning themselves.

Since iguanid species are becoming popular with hobbyists, there is a growing legion of herpetoculturists turning out beautiful, domestically bred specimens. Lizard shown is Grand Cayman Island Ground Iguana, *Cyclura nubila nubila*.

BILL CHRISTIE